HIDDEN WARFARE

David Watson

STL BOOKS

PO Box 48, Bromley, Kent, England

© 1972 David C K Watson as
God's Freedom Fighters, published by Movements Books (Send The
Light Trust)

Revised edition published by Harold Shaw Publishers,
Box 567, Wheaton, Illinois 60187, USA, as How to Win the War, 1979.
Revised by Mel Lorentzen. This edition 1980

STL Books are published by
Sent The Light Trust,
9 London Road, Bromley, Kent, England

ISBN 0 903843 39 0

Printed and bound in Great Britain by
Cox & Wyman Ltd, Reading

Contents

To Anne, my fellow-freedom-fighter

Acknowledgements

The author acknowledges gratefully much guidance from Dr. Martyn Lloyd-Jones, who, in Westminster Chapel from 1960 to 1962, preached on "The Christian Warfare". Some of the material in this book was stimulated by those sermons.

He also is very grateful to the staff of The Movement for World Evangelization for their help in preparing the manuscript. In particular, he is grateful to Mr. John Fear, the Director of Administration of M.W.E., for all his encouragement and guidance. He is grateful as well to Miss Frances Smith in her careful reading of the manuscript.

He also wishes to thank members of St. Cuthbert's Church, York, for their fellowship, love and prayer in many of the spiritual battles of the last few years.

All Scripture quotations, unless otherwise indicated, are from the Revised Standard Version of the Bible.

Introduction

While most people in their weariness from the devastation of wars in this 20th century express a keen desire for world peace, they remain fascinated by the subject of war. Thriving veterans' organizations, best-selling memoirs of military heroes, endless television re-runs of war movies and the space-age craze for games that simulate inter-galactic combat—all these reinforce an instinctive human obsession with competition and conquest. The sports-minded public spends incredible millions of pounds annually to indulge its passion for watching professional athletes contend for championship titles. In the spheres of commerce, politics and high society, the drive to dominate by defeating all opponents motivates widespread strategic planning and effort.

Should it seem incongruous then to speak of warfare in a spiritual sense? It is a concept that the human mind can readily comprehend. The metaphors of war occur frequently and prominently in the New Testament, even in such a startling utterance by the Lord Jesus Christ: "I have not come to bring peace, but a sword" (Matthew 10:34).

We need to look carefully, then, at the whole theme of Christian warfare in the light of three truths which have increasingly impressed themselves on my mind.

The intense reality of this warfare

The Apostle Paul instructed the early Christians about the contending forces which are in combat in the world and, indeed, in our very souls. To the young believers at Ephesus he wrote:

> And you he made alive when you were dead through the trespasses and sins in which you once walked, following the course of this world, following the prince of the power of the air, the spirit that is now at work in the sons of disobedience. Among these we all once lived in the passions of our flesh, following the desires of body and mind, and so we were by nature children of wrath, like the rest of mankind. But God, who is rich in mercy, out of the great love with which he loved us, even when we were dead through our trespasses, made us alive together with Christ (by grace you have been saved), and raised us up with him, and made us sit with him in the heavenly places in Christ Jesus, that in the coming ages he might show the immeasur-

able riches of his grace in kindness toward us in Christ Jesus.

Before the Ephesians believed in Christ, Paul explains, they were spiritually dead because of their sins. While in that condition they were following: the course of this world, the prince of the power of the air and the desires of body and mind, or the passions of the flesh. The corrupt lifestyle of the heathen, the leadership of Satan and the self-indulgent gratification of natural instincts characterized their existence.

However, Paul writes, God's great love and mercy brought them into spiritual life, rescued them from death through the grace and triumph of Christ himself. Incredibly, he has even installed them as integral parts of Christ's own hierarchy of authority, allowing them to share in it as a demonstration of the lavishness of divine generosity.

A believer in Christ, therefore, has *changed sides*. He has left the devil's team and joined God's. To put it more biblically, he has been redeemed or bought back from captivity to Satan and set free by Christ to join the ranks in battle against his former tyrannical master. In Ephesians 6:12, Paul clearly defines the nature of the battle:

> For we are not contending against flesh and blood, but against the principalities, against the powers, against the world rulers of this present darkness, against the spiritual hosts of wickedness in heavenly places.

During the detailed preparation of these chapters, we have seen, in our own family in particular, and to some extent in our church, just how real this warfare is. The devil does not like to be exposed!

The marked increase of Satanic activity

Not too long ago, the devil's doings were kept pretty much below the surface of civilized society's consciousness. Now all that has changed. A widespread and intense interest in occult powers and practices confronts us everywhere. School and college students use ouija boards and tarot cards seriously. Sophisticated society people attend seances. Popular magazines feature articles about black and white magic and profile the lives of well-known seers and prophets. Newspapers provide daily astrology readings and broad coverage of cults that worship Satan. In England alone, one recent report estimated that there were 2,500 practicing witches and in the United States some churches have had to keep their doors locked or guarded during the week to prevent devil cultists from sneaking in to perform blasphemous mock communion rites on Christian altars.

Such realities make obvious the urgent need for Christians to be better equipped for all-out war on Satan.

The sad ignorance of many Christians

Although Christians *theoretically* acknowledge that

Satan is God's enemy, a real and active spiritual being, by their casual attitude toward hell's activities they seem to have forgotten that it is their God-given commission to fight him.

In pastoral work, I am often almost overwhelmed by what I call "Christian casualties." All too frequently one meets fine Christians who are unnaturally depressed, defeated or oppressed by unrecognized dark powers, or who are suddenly filled with doubts or bitterness. They are unaware that they are in need of deliverance. They need to be freed from Satan's power.

A missionary leader in Thailand told me some years ago that about 50% of the missionaries in that land had been invalided out because of breakdowns and illness. He said: "I believe it is because we are largely ignorant of this spiritual warfare."

In 1968, Robert Peterson of the Overseas Missionary Fellowship published his book, *Roaring Lion*. In the preface, he commented that when he came to this country to speak of some of the demonic activities which he had observed in Borneo, not only did people not understand what he was saying, but they refused to believe him. "These are nothing but hallucinations, fantastic dreams," they said. Peterson comments: "The Old Testament deals with demonic activity in many of its aspects. Christ regarded demonism as a stern reality. The writers of the Epistles spared no efforts in their exposure of these evil forces. Today we see the foolish heart of man darkened by the ceaseless activity of this host of seducing spirits. Can we in all honesty then let the 'hallucination' statement above go by without challenge? I think not!" He adds: "My prayer is that this book will help the Christian to know a little better 'the depths of Satan' and by knowing, to help him 'fight the good fight of faith.' "

That is my prayer for this book. There are few subjects which seem to be so little understood as this. Such ignorance plays into Satan's hands. For us to know our enemy and his tactics is the beginning of our sharing in God's victory over him through the Lord Jesus Christ.

War Declared!

1

"I will put enmity between you" *Genesis 3:15.*

Planet Earth, as our globe is often called, is a battleground. Beyond all of the isolated guerilla skirmishes and territorial border clashes that we hear about, even beyond the occasional devastating world wars, a struggle rages constantly, inflicting more destruction than that which could be produced by neutron bombs or even more unthinkable secret weapons. Hostilities on the spiritual front are making the world a holocaust.

This deadly conflict is contrary to God's original design in the creation of our world. To comprehend the magnitude and scope of spiritual warfare we need to be aware of the divine plan for this earth, both before and after things went wrong.

1. Beautiful Beginnings

Until recently, we humans knew little about the earth's physical appearance apart from a generally hazy concept of the outlines of oceans and continents. Map-makers traditionally differentiated between countries and states by using different colors. Yet passengers in a jumbo jet look down from a 30,000 foot altitude on landscapes that are relatively drab and monotonous. When J. B. Phillips whimsically described an angel's view of the earth, he likened it to a dirty tennis ball. Environmental pollution is alarming the experts. Does physical desolation and ugliness have to be the price of technological "progress?"

Everyone was more or less startled, therefore, when the astronauts who were probing space transmitted back photographs of a glowing, almost iridescent globe and spoke in awed tones of the beauty of the "earthshine."

Bible students should not have been surprised at such a discovery. The creation record of Genesis 1 and 2 reveals three fundamental facts:

First, God created the heavens and the earth (Genesis 1:1). Since he is absolute goodness in himself, anything derived from his power and intelligence is bound to be good also. The Creator could not create confusion!

Second, God himself bore witness that everything he had made was very good (Genesis 1:31). Dualism falsely claims that only spirit is good, that matter is evil and that the two are irreconcilably opposed to each other. The Bible says that the earth, and plant life and animal life and the human race are all declared *good* by their Maker.

Finally, God planned the earth to be the residence for his highest created beings, humans whom he made in his own image (Genesis 1:27; 2:7, 8), and whom he put in charge of the rest of creation (Genesis 1:28; 2:15; Psalm 8:6-8).

Indeed, God's creation is for our benefit and for our enjoyment. Yet since he is the original source of life, we remain forever dependent on him. God meant that dependence to be a beautiful relationship of love between the creature and his loving Creator God; we were supposed to enjoy each other's company (Genesis 3:8, 9).

The physical world is not only a part of the immeasurable solar system, it is also a place under God's rule. Why, then, is our planet the scene of destruction, pain and corruption? What has disfigured it? What went wrong?

2. Catastrophe and Corruption

All the fresh and glorious environment of their garden paradise were Adam and Eve's to enjoy. That in itself might have been a temptation to careless independence of God. To continually remind them that he was the source of their life and the head of the hierarchy of authority, God set one restriction: they were not to eat fruit from one specified tree (Genesis 2:16, 17). Disobedience meant death—first a cutting of the spiritual life-bond between them and their Creator, and eventually physical death. All that—and something else—came horribly true when they ignored God's instructions and ate the forbidden fruit, at Satan's suggestion.

The barrier

Human sin has built a barrier between man and God. As soon as Adam and Eve realized what they had done, they foolishly tried to hide from God (Genesis 3:8). When the Lord found them (as was inevitable) he confirmed the rupture of the relationship by expelling them from the garden and by assigning angelic beings with a flaming sword to prevent access to the tree of life (Genesis 3:23, 24). They had brought upon themselves the judgment of God.

Ever since, the human race has missed that close friendship with God which man was created to enjoy. One of the obvious symptoms of the emptiness of today's society is its spiritual appetite for the transcendent, for spiritual reality. While there is actually a hunger for God resulting from a famine of personal experience of God's reality, many are finding a spurious substitute for God in the powers of evil.

The power shift

Another consequence of man's disobedience to God makes the condition even more complicated, for human sin brought the world itself under Satan's control. God's Kingdom of Light became Satan's Kingdom of Darkness—characterized by perversity, suffering, sickness and death. Although we may not understand the precise mechanics of the transaction, the fact remains: because man was given dominion and stewardship over the world, when man fell, the world fell; when man gave over his control to Satan, the world came under Satan's manipulation. All of Scripture reflects and acknowledges this tragic situation.

> The Lord saw that the wickedness of man was great in the earth, and that every imagination of the thoughts of his heart was only evil continually. And the Lord was sorry that he had made man on the earth, and it grieved him to his heart (Genesis 6:5, 6).

The apostles had their comments on this prevalent condition: John said, "The whole world is in the power of the evil one." James observed that "friendship with the world is enmity with God." And according to Paul the "creation is in bondage to decay and it groans for redemption."

What did John means by "the whole world?" A clearer understanding of what this includes is urgently needed. Remember, the world is a battleground. Satan, the enemy, has invaded and occupied God's rightful territory. It is all too easy to fit our thinking into the following framework: on the one hand we have "the Christian Church" with its blessings and patterns of worship; far away on the horizon is "the world" with its drugs and drinks and gambling and illicit sex and dishonesty; and in between is the harmless "no man's land" with its ordinary activities—eating, drinking, sleeping, working. Of course, such things are not wrong in themselves, but we should recognize that they *belong* to the universal system controlled by Satan.

Therefore, "the *whole* world" which is under Satan's control must include the world of education, the world of relationships, the world of philosophy, the world of politics, the world of entertainment, the world of radio and television, the world of the printed page. No dimension of human existence and experience is exempt from the distortion and damaging force of Satan's domination.

We see this in the standards, the value system of the world which touches us insidiously every day. For instance, think about the popular definitions of love that are reflected in media advertising: "Love is romance in the Bahamas." "Love is a diamond." "Love is a bottle of French perfume." Success is measured in terms of property holdings, position in a corporate hierarchy, a winter vacation in the French Riviera, or membership in an exclusive country club. Jesus asked: "What shall it profit a man if he gains the whole world and loses his own soul?" It is that "whole world" that is in the power of the evil one and that reflects the distorted and malevolent values of its ruler.

Ordinary life: All of life?
Remember Jesus' words? "As it was in the days of

Noah, so will it be in the days of the Son of man. They ate, they drank, they married, they were given in marriage" (Luke 17:26, 26). Notice the items on that list. Jesus did not say that the people in Noah's day lusted or fornicated or gambled or defrauded. No, they were involved in perfectly acceptable activities until the day "when Noah entered the ark, and the flood came and destroyed them all." Then Jesus went on to describe the days of Lot: "they ate, they drank, they bought, they sold, they planted, they built"— again, all the components of ordinary living. Yet, "on the day when Lot went out from Sodom fire and brimstone rained from heaven and destroyed them all."

If Jesus was describing natural, everyday activities (though the people probably lusted and bribed as well!) why did God's judgment fall on them? Because these things were *all* they lived for, their *whole* life, their *whole* world. And never forget, it is that "whole world" that is in the power of the evil one.

The problem for the Christian is not how to avoid buying and selling, eating and drinking, marrying and giving in marriage—these are all integral parts of human existence. The basic problem is how to avoid being controlled by *the power behind these things,* the power of the evil one himself.

There is only one answer to this problem that seems clear in Scripture: as Christians we must handle these routine activities for the glory of God alone. Remember the example of Johann Sebastian Bach, who inscribed every musical score, sacred or secular, with the words *soli gloria Deo*—"to God alone be glory." Therefore, our activities belong either to God, if we can do them to his glory, or to Satan. Remember that in the parable of the sower, Jesus described the seed that fell among thorns like this: "They are those who hear, but as they go on their way they are choked by the cares and riches and pleasures of life"—ordinary things used by Satan to spoil God's work.

"Oh," says someone, "I must have that dress (or that record, or that car). I *must* have it." Must you? have you prayed about it? Are you buying it for God's glory? You may retort that you don't pray about such things. But you should, because when you are handling the things of this world you may well be coming under the power that controls it all. Even with the most ordinary decisions and activities, our lives should be so centered in Christ and his glory that our choices and actions contribute to his kingdom, not Satan's.

The balance of the Bible
The Scriptures, far from being negative, provide a beautiful balance for living. In 1 Timothy 4:1-3 Paul writes:

> Now the Spirit expressly says that in later

times some will depart from the faith by giving heed to deceitful spirits and doctrines of demons, through the pretensions of liars whose consciences are seared, who forbid marriage and enjoin abstinence from foods which God created to be received with thanksgiving by those who believe and know the truth.

In other words, an excessively negative attitude to the world ("Don't do this; don't do that") might even be a doctrine of demons! And Paul goes on: "For everything created by God is good, and nothing is to be rejected *if it is received with thanksgiving;* for then it is consecrated by the word of God and prayer."

If we live our ordinary lives for the glory of God, if we pray about what we do, if we receive his gifts with thanksgiving, *then* they are consecrated by the word of God and prayer, and they are good and beautiful and wholesome in God's sight.

Now, bearing in mind that the whole world is under Satan's control, two facts follow.

The world refuses to know God
The world rejects God's Son: "He was in the world, and the world was made through him, yet the world knew him not." It also rejects God's Holy Spirit and is determined to exist independently of his guidance. And that is the constant, unremitting effort of the Enemy—to make us

think we can live independently, that in ourselves we have adequate resources, that we don't really *need* God, that we have "come of age" at last.

In a very important passage about the world, Paul writes to the Christians at Corinth, "Where is the wise man? Where is the scribe? Where is the debater of this age? Has not God made foolish the wisdom of the world? For since, in the wisdom of God, the world did not know God through wisdom, it pleased God through the folly of what we preach to save those who believe. For Jews demand signs and Greeks seek wisdom, but we preach Christ crucified, a stumbling block to Gentiles, but to those who are called, both Jews and Greeks, Christ the power of God and the wisdom of God" (1 Corinthians 1:20-24). Here, both Jew and Gentile are shown to prefer the wisdom and the power of the world to the wisdom and power of God.

The Jew—the religious man
Part of the deception of this world is that it may offer us a form of religion while denying its power. In Colossians 2 Paul writes: "If with Christ you died to the elemental spirits of the universe, why do you live as if you still belonged to the world? Why do you submit to regulations, 'Do not handle, do not taste, do not touch" (referring to *things* which all perish as they are used), according to human precepts and doctrines? These have indeed an appearance of wisdom in promoting

rigor of devotion and self-abasement and severity to the body, but they are of no value in checking the indulgence of the flesh (Colossians 2:20-23). What the world says is something like this: "If you want religion you can have religion." So the world offers us legalism or asceticism or ritual or organization—anything which superficially resembles spirituality but which in fact is quite useless—a counterfeit of the real thing.

Structure or spiritual power?

You can sketch a fairly accurate picture of the history of the Church like this: God gave a wonderful, fresh breath of Holy Spirit life (on the day of Pentecost, and repeatedly, during church renewal down the centuries) and man comes along and says, "Wonderful! Now, let's set up a Church Preservation Society to keep things going." And he begins to organize a new denomination, a new fellowship, a different structure, fresh rules and regulations and activities, during which the Holy Spirit quietly (and often unnoticed) makes his departure. Does this new, forward-looking framework collapse overnight? Not a bit of it! It goes on, year after year, even century after century—the world's counterfeit of the real thing.

A great prophet of the 20th century, A. W. Tozer, expressed it like this:

> "The Church began in power, moved in power, and moved just as long as she had power. When she no longer had power she

dug in for safety and sought to conserve her
gains. But her blessings were like manna;
though they tried to keep it overnight it bred
worms and stank. So we have had monasti-
cism, scholasticism, institutionalism, and
they have all been indicative of the same
thing: absence of spiritual power.[1]

When I moved to York in 1965 we came to one
of the twelve "redundant" churches in that city.
Now what could we do with an empty, redundant
Church? We decided to have, apart from the very
simple structure of Sunday services, only one
organization: one mid-week meeting for Bible
study and prayer. In the very early days there
were about five people, I think, who started to
come to this. Four years later we still had only this
one organized meeting for Bible study and for
prayer; we had no Sunday School, no Youth
Group, no Young Wives' Club, no Mothers'
Union, no Men's Group, none of the organizations common to most churches. And some of my
colleagues were saying to me "How can your
church exist without a Sunday School? How can
you possibly manage without a Mother's Union?"
But we felt very strongly that we would not make
any move at all in establishing organizations until
the Spirit of God made it abundantly clear to us.
We knew that "unless the Lord builds the house,
those who build it labor in vain."

I am not for one moment suggesting that every

church should scrap all its organizations. But the danger is that these organizations can come into existence for a real purpose, but can become self-perpetuating, can roll along on their own momentum even though the vital spark of the Spirit's power has died out; then they belong to the world because they have lost their spiritual purpose. Watchman Nee, in his helpful book *Love Not the World,* says: "The Church depends for its very existence upon a ceaseless impartation of fresh life from God, and cannot survive one day without it."[2] Therefore, if a church or fellowship or organization ceases to depend upon the Spirit of God for constant fresh life, it dies and becomes a part of the world—holding a *form* of religion, sound, even evangelical—but denying the power of God. You can find too many churches today which are "sound," but sound asleep, lacking the life and power of the Spirit which is so vital in our life for God and in the advance of his kingdom.

In student missions I have found repeatedly that the main obstacle to personal faith in Christ in an individual is the established, organized Church! Over and over again I find this thrown at me. I am not speaking of one particular denomination. But we must confess that the church as a whole has offered people *religion,* the world's counterfeit, rather than Christ and the power of the Spirit.

The Gentile—the secular man
If the Jew represents the religious man, the Gen-

tile represents his secular counterpart, the rationalist who depends on learning, logic, philosophy and argument. Once again, this is the spirit of the world which rejects Jesus Christ the Wisdom of God. Paul says "Jews demand signs and Greeks seek wisdom, but we preach Christ crucified, a stumbling block to Jews and folly to Gentiles." He further expands on this in 1 Corinthians 2: "When I came to you, brethren, I did not come proclaiming to you the testimony of God in lofty words or wisdom. For I decided to know *nothing* among you except Jesus Christ and him crucified. And I was with you in weakness and in much fear and trembling; and my speech and my message were not in plausible words of wisdom, but in demonstration of the Spirit and power, that your faith might not rest in the wisdom of men, but in the power of God" (1 Corinthians 2:1-5).

Let me illustrate this. I owe an enormous personal benefit to the work of Francis Schaeffer, and I have a great respect for God's work at L'Abri. What is the purpose of L'Abri? Edith Schaeffer explains it in her book, *L'Abri*,[3] "to show forth by demonstration in our life and work the existence of God." She goes on to say what she means by this, "We have set forth to live by prayer in these four specific realms:

> 1. We make our financial and material needs known to God alone, in prayer, rather than sending out pleas for money. . . .

2. We pray that God will bring the people of his choice to us, and keep all others away. . . .
3. We pray that God will plan the work and unfold his plan to us day by day. . . .
4. We pray that God will send the workers of his choice to us, rather than pleading for workers in the usual channels."

You see that it is God, God, God. God-centered, not man-organized; and that is no doubt why God seems unmistakably to be blessing that particular work. Here is a fellowship which depends on God for its daily spiritual life. But it is dangerously possible for some Christians to take Schaeffer's learning and Schaeffer's philosophy and Schaeffer's interpretation of history and culture and Schaeffer's insights without Schaeffer's *prayer;* and then it becomes the world's counterfeit. Indeed it may become the exact opposite of what Paul says when he claims that he came to Corinth in "demonstration of the Spirit and power, that your faith might not rest in the wisdom of men but in the power of God."

Pro-man; not pro-God
In one university mission that I was leading, there was a residence hall that housed an "ultra-Schaeffer" group. They were critical about the organization of the mission and argumentative in the discussions. Significantly, they showed no sign whatever of God's blessing! It was a tragic

illustration of the spirit of the world which all the time seeks to force us to work and live independently of God. This is no criticism of Dr. Francis Schaeffer but an example of what may happen if our trust is in man instead of God. And I have been disturbed recently by a number of evangelical conferences and organizations and committees whose emphasis is more on strategy than on prayer. Unless we pray we are wasting our time. When we work, *we* work. When we pray then *God* can work. It is all too easy to imbibe the spirit of the world, either refusing to acknowledge God at all, or refusing to depend on him for everything.

However, the world not only refuses to know God; it requires the worship of man. Because of this John warns his readers, "Do not love the world or the things in the world. If anyone loves the world, love for the Father is not in him. For all that is in the world, the lust of the flesh and the lust of the eyes and the pride of life, is not of the Father but is of the world" (1 John 2:15-16). That, of course, is a reference to the original temptation of man in Genesis 3. Almost exactly the same expressions are used there. Satan knew that if Adam and Eve could become victims of the lust of the flesh and the lust of the eyes and the pride of life, desiring to be like God and to know as God knows, then man would worship and serve Satan, as well as Satan's world from that moment on. Thus, in Paul's letter to the Romans, you see the appalling picture of man in utter bondage to the world: "They exchanged the truth about God for a lie and worshipped and served the creature rather than the Creator" (Romans 1:25).

Travellers once came to an island and found a tribe of moon-worshippers. The travellers said, "This is strange. If you really want to worship something in the sky, why don't you worship the sun rather than the moon?" They were told, "It's very simple—the sun shines only by day, when it's light and we don't need it; but the moon shines at night when it's dark and we cannot see!" They failed to realize that the light of the moon derives entirely from the light of the sun. The belief resulted from ignorance! Yet today most people worship the creature rather than the Creator. They ignore the Source of everything and worship its products.

It's not surprising, then, that man is left without answers to the great questions of today. In the musical *Hair* there is one refrain which keeps on pleading, "Tell me why, tell me why, tell me why. Is there an answer? Tell me why." If man today is lost, it is the inevitable result of living in a world which refuses to recognize or know God, which requires the worship of man. If Satan's control of this world were the end of the story, the human dilemma would indeed be hopeless. The existentialists would be right in calling our life here on earth an absurdity.

But while the world is undeniably Satan-controlled, it is decidedly *not* God-forsaken!

3. New People, New Purpose

Remember how much the earth and the human race meant to God when he created them in the beginning? Do you think he would turn his back both on the Creation which he called *very good,* and on man, formed in his own image to enjoy fellowship with him? No, indeed! Rather it was man who turned his back on God. When God came seeking Adam and Eve, they ran away into hiding. Even to this day, the Lord continues his mighty counteroffensive against Satan by searching for sinners (Luke 19:10).

God, because he is the Creator and rightful sovereign over his creation, is eternally determined to reclaim his territory and redeem the rebels. Even at the moment he was sentencing Adam and Eve to their punishment, he decreed Satan's destruction by a coming deliverer (Genesis 3:15).

The apostle Paul expounded this marvelous truth as the Holy Spirit instructed him, identifying Christ Jesus as the promised deliverer:

> All this is from God, who through Christ reconciled us to himself and give us the ministry of reconciliation; that is, God was in Christ reconciling the world to himself, not counting their trespasses against them, and entrusting to us the message of reconcilia-

tion. So we are ambassadors for Christ, God making his appeal through us. We beseech you on behalf of Christ, be reconciled to God (2 Corinthians 5:18-20).

As ambassadors, our assignment is to bring the world back to God, to take control of it away from Satan by the power of Jesus.

In Christ, in the world
What is our place, then, as Christians in this world which is in the power of the wicked one? We are *in Christ,* in the world.

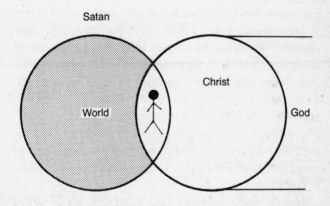

In this overlapping position, *in Christ in the world,* we are safe not only from the pull of the world power of Satan (provided we *abide* in Christ) but we are also in that strategic position to reconcile the world to God.

One Baptist minister gave the following charge to his son who was being ordained into the Baptist ministry: "Ted, my son, keep close to God. Ted, my son, keep close to man. Ted, my son, bring God and men together."[4] That is a wonderful charge, and it illustrates the delicate balance that we need to maintain in order to fulfill effectively the ministry of reconciliation entrusted by God into our hands.

Don't be squeezed into the world's mould

However, it is obvious that we can make one of two mistakes. First, *we may keep close to man but fail to stay close to God.* Then what happens? Immediately, we become vulnerable. Paul tells us in Romans 12:2 (J. B. Phillips translates it so vividly), "Don't let the world around you squeeze you into its own mould, but let God remold your minds from within." How? By "presenting your bodies" everyday as a "living sacrifice." In other words, we must daily abide in Jesus, obedient, yielded, in touch. Anything less in our relationship leaves us open to the enemy's wiles.

Here I want to be very frank, at the risk of being misunderstood. In evangelical circles it is common to refer to a Christian as "worldly" is he smokes or dranks or gambles or goes to the pictures. A "non-worldly," spiritual Christian is, by this definition, one who doesn't smoke, doesn't abuse drugs, doesn't drink, doesn't gamble, doesn't frequent cinemas. But my conviction is that these rules and guidelines, by *themselves,* are no protection from the world at all. I may never smoke, I may never drink, I may never do any of a number of suspect activities and yet, in the New Testament sense, I could still be a thoroughly worldly Christian! That may surprise you. But the crucial question for me to ask is this: "Is the emphasis of my life on *things*— doing things or not doing them—or is the focal point of my life Jesus Christ?" I must ask that question every day. Remember that the string of "don't do's", that legalistic attitude, is the world's counterfeit of the real thing. The *real thing* is a living, fresh, vital walk with Jesus Christ day by day.

Turning again to Colossians 2, Paul here exhorts the Christians that as they have "received Christ Jesus the Lord, so live in him, rooted and built up in him." Therefore, he asks, why do you submit to regulations, "Do not handle, do not taste, do not touch (referring to *things* which all perish as they are used)?" These things may have an appearance of spirituality but by themselves they are quite futile. Therefore, says Paul, "If then you have been raised with Christ, seek the things that are above, where Christ is, seated at the right hand of God. Set your minds on things that are above, not on things that are on earth. For you have died, and your life is hid with Christ in God" (Colossians 2:6, 20-22; 3:1-3).

Satan's subtle deception

Perhaps now you can see Satan's strategy, and why many evangelical Christians or churches or fellowships have lost their spiritual power and vision even though they are very careful about what they do or don't do. Satan can be so subtle. He suggests something like this: "I see that most Christians do not smoke, or drink, or gamble, etc. (so often we *do* have better things to do with our time and money anyway) so I'll convince them that these things they don't do are the very essence of spiritual living. Provided they keep these rules, they are safe." Thus he lures us out of security of abiding in Christ and we concentrate on going to lots of church meetings and we don't do this and we don't do that, and soon he has created a worldly Christian because our preoccupation is with *things* instead of with Jesus.

Let me illustrate this from my experience, in our church, with a young professional actress who was wonderfully born again. She came to see me shortly after her conversion and asked, "Well, now that I have found Christ, do you think that I should give up my acting?" I realized immediately that Satan was tempting her to live the Christian life by rules and regulations; so I said, "No, don't give up your acting, but seek to deepen your relationship with Jesus and let him guide you step by step."

All was well with her for a number of months, but one day she called me up in great distress, crying on the other end of the phone. The one producer who could "make her or break her", who was getting her important parts and could do so in the future, wanted her to act in a play which, although not actually obscene, was still rather casual about sexual relationships. As a Christian, she felt very uncomfortable about taking a part in this play. "If I try to tell him that I can't do it, he won't understand," she sobbed. "He'll be furious. What should I do?"

Again, I felt it would be wrong for *me* to tell her what to do. I suggested, "You go and talk to the Lord Jesus about it and you let the peace of Christ in your heart be your guide as you pray about it. *He* will guide you. I can't tell you what to do. *I* don't know! But he does!" I concluded our conversations with the reminder from 1 Samuel 2:30, "Those that honor me, I will honor."

A few days later she wrote to me the following letter: "Dear David, I prayed about my work and God would not even let me *think* about doing that play. So I rang the director who, of course, was furious, could not understand my point of view, told me I was a rank amateur, and that he couldn't waste time trying to help me, etc. But while he was speaking, I felt so wonderful, *as if Jesus was smiling down on me,* a wonderful radiance difficult to describe." She went on, "I have a great feeling of joy and I'm so glad to be able to do something for my God. I'll put my trust in him for my work and for everything." A few days later she heard that she was being offered a part in a film, a part that was exciting, glorifying to God and better in every way. God always honors those who honor him. The peace of God, as promised, was ruling in her heart.

Keep in touch

The other mistake we may make, as we try to live as Christians in the world, is that we may *keep so close to God,* or rather the things of God, *that we fail to stay in touch with man, and his needs.* We may become so involved with Christian activities and Christian meetings that we lose any meaningful contact with those who are still outside of Christ. Leighton Ford, in his fine book, *Good News is For Sharing,* says this: "Part of Jesus' attractiveness, which drew secular people like a magnet, was his wonderful love of life, his natural appealing friendliness. Luke shows Jesus going from dinner party to dinner party, teaching the Gospel to all the guests. If Jesus came back today and mingled with gamblers, the skid-row crowd and the cocktail set, a lot of shocked Christians would throw up their hands and say he was too worldly!"[5]

Certainly it is not easy to keep this balance between really knowing God and loving him day by day, and knowing man and his needs, his agonies and his loneliness. Therefore Jesus, knowing all about the difficulties in achieving this balance, prayed for his disciples like this: "I have given them thy word; and the world has hated them because they are not of the world, even as I am not of the world. I do not pray that thou shouldst take them out of the world, but that thou shouldst keep them from the evil one. They are not of the world, even as I am not of the world. Sanctify them in the truth; thy word is truth. As thou didst send me into the world, so I have sent them into the world. And for their sake I consecrate myself, that they also may be consecrated in truth. I do not pray for these only, but also for those who believe in me through their word" (John 17:14-20).

No holes in the boat
This is the vital thing, that we should be *in* the world but not *of* the world. Just as a boat should be in the water but the water should not be in the boat, so a Christian should be in the world but the world should not be in that Christian. And for the sake of those for whom Christ died and who are going to believe on him through our word, we should sanctify ourselves, and maintain our determination to abide in him. There is no other place of safety and power.

Generally speaking, we will probably not want to spend a large proportion of our time on "worldly amusements." We have found something far more satisfying in the unsearchable riches of Christ. But if we really love him, there may be times when we can safely find ourselves in situations, or with certain people, that might surprise some other Christians.

In that case, there are two things for us to watch very carefully: First, "Take care lest this liberty of yours somehow become a stumbling block to the weak" (1 Corinthians 8:9). Then, "Let any one who thinks that he stands take heed lest he fall" (1 Corinthians 10:12). An electrician may handle a "live" wire. If he knows what he is doing and takes adequate precautions, he will be quite safe. So it is with the Christian and the world.

The over-riding question that remains is: How will it all turn out? Is the world to be constantly tossed back and forth between God and Satan? Is this battle a see-saw that could tilt either way?

4. Our Fabulous Future

God never meant us to have a moment's doubt as to the outcome of the Christian's warfare against Satan and his power in this world. In the thick of the battle, as we fight against an entrenched enemy, we have this assurance: the Captain of our salvation, Jesus Christ, has already won the battle. He invaded death and hell, disarmed the enemy, opened prison doors and set the captives free. The war we are fighting is simply a mop-up operation against Satan's "last ditch" defenses on our way to the victory celebration with our Lord. When the war is over, he will make the earth new and will rule over it as King of kings, with us by his side.

What does that future prospect mean for us here and now on the battleground of this world? It means that we won't let ourselves be fooled by the seeming toughness of the devil's strongholds, and we won't let ourselves get tangled in his power structures right on the brink of their destruction.

You see, the present "world" is temporary. It is passing away. If I knew that a certain large commercial concern was soon to be liquidated, I would certainly not invest money in it. I could expect not profit on my investment. I would refuse to get involved.

Since this world is going to pass away, why get too involved with it? Paul wrote: "God forbid that I should boast about anything or anybody except the cross of our Lord Jesus Christ, which means that *the world is a dead thing to me and I am a dead man to the world!*" (Galatians 6:14, *Phillips*).

Christians will not get involved and tied up with the ways of the world because all their deepest needs find a more lasting, a closer, a more satisfying answer in walking with Christ. His forgiveness, peace, love, assurance—and life—are things that this world can never give. At the cross, God himself becomes real to us as we hand ourselves over, give ourselves back to our rightful Lord and accept his commission to fight against the devil and all his works, in Jesus' name!

Three guidelines

If a Christian has doubts or questions about how to discern "right and wrong" in relating to the daily necessities of living in this world, here are three practical principles that have often helped me:

First, will what I want to do help or hinder my relationship with Jesus? (Hebrews 12:1, 2) Then, will it help or hinder someone else's relationship with Jesus? (1 Corinthians 8:9) Above all, finally, will it glorify God? (1 Corinthians 10:31-11:1)

Our warfare is against the world, the flesh and the devil. The world, this earth on which we live, is the scene of the battle because it is temporarily dominated by the controlling power of that diabolical invader, Satan. But his destiny is total defeat and oblivion. That is why he is so desperately trying to demonstrate his powers in the short time he has left. We must look much more closely at his strategies and discuss his tactics further in this book, but next we shall turn our attention to the requirements for being one of God's fighters in this battle.

Notes

[1] A. W. Tozer, *Paths to Power*, (Great Britain: Marshall Morgan & Scott).

[2] Watchman Nee, *Love Not The World*, (Christian Literature Crusade, 1970).

[3] Edith Schaeffer, *L'Abri*, (Great Britain: Norfolk Press).

[4] Quoted by Leighton Ford in *The Christian Persuader*, (New York: Harper & Row, 1966).

[5] *Ibid.*

Fighter Qualifications

2

"No soldier on service gets entangled in civilian pursuits" *2 Timothy 2:4*.

In spite of all the sophisticated weaponry developed by the modern military-industrial complex, warfare still requires man-power—troops. The world's super-powers may confer about strategic arms limitation agreements, but they still maintain huge standing armies and trained reserve units.

For the spiritual conflict with Satan, God too recruits and trains his own fighting forces: Christians make up the army of the Lord on earth. In the heavenly realms, he deploys legions of angels and archangels, of cherubim and seraphim. In this world, he primarily uses men and women specially picked and prepared. They are people who have been reborn spiritually, made partakers of divine life, and endowed by the Holy Spirit with particular individual abilities to serve Christ's cause.

Granting all of that we must also admit that as soldiers of the cross most of us are, to a considerable degree, "raw recruits." We have a lot to learn about campaigning in enemy-occupied territory. The Lord made this acutely clear to the Apostle Paul as he was writing his letter to believers living in Rome.

> For those who live according to the flesh set their minds on the things of the flesh, but those who live according to the Spirit set their minds on the things of the Spirit. To set the mind on the flesh is death, but to set the mind on the Spirit is life and peace. For the mind that is set on the flesh is hostile to God; it does not submit to God's law, indeed it cannot; and those who are in the flesh cannot please God (Romans 8:5-9).

1. The "Self" Center

A definition of the term "the flesh" is crucial to an understanding of the uniqueness of the Lord's army. Sometimes in the Scriptures of course, "the flesh" refers to human physical existence. In that sense, on at least three occasions in the New Testament, Jesus Christ himself is described on earth as being "in the flesh." 1 John 4:2, for example: "Every spirit which confesses that Jesus Christ has come in the flesh is of God."

In Romans 8, however, the word "flesh" means something quite different. Paul writes regarding Christians, "you are not in the flesh, you are in the Spirit" (verse 9). Obviously, the word cannot refer there to the physical body. Rather, it signifies our selflife, our own natural, selfish and self-preserving instincts and inclinations, our earthly nature with all of its ingrained lusts and desires.

Self

One very simple way of remembering what the word "flesh" means is to spell it out—F L E S H —then knock off the last letter, H, and read the letters in reverse: S E L F !

In Galatians 5:19-21, Paul describes the natural expressions of the "flesh":

> When you follow your own wrong inclinations your lives will produce these evil results: impure thoughts, eagerness for lustful pleasure, idolatry, spiritism, hatred and fighting, jealousy and anger, constant effort to get the best for yourself, complaints and criticisms, the feeling that everyone else is wrong except those in your own little group . . . envy, murder, drunkenness, wild parties and all that sort of thing. Let me tell you again . . . that anyone living that sort of life will not inherit the kingdom of God (*The Living Bible*).

In his book, *The Spirit of the Living God,*[1] Leon Morris gives an illustration of the flesh in terms of a young married couple going through a time of crisis. The wife was about to leave her husband, and at the husband's request, the local minister went over to see her. He tried to persuade her to stay with her spouse, but she answered: "Nothing that you can say will shake my determination. I no longer love my husband. Life with him would be inexpressibly dreary. I have a right to be happy, and I mean to claim that right."

Dr. Morris comments, "Those words, 'I have a right to be happy,' perfectly express the mind of the flesh. No matter at what cost to others, no matter at what ultimate cost to himself, the fleshly person claims the right to be happy. For the selfish individual, all other considerations must be subordinate to that."

Five facts about the flesh

In Romans 8, Paul describes the self-centered life. First, the flesh has weakened the law (verse 3). Because of our self-life, the law of God, although good and right and perfect, cannot make man right with God and cannot help man to overcome sin. God's law is a standard set by his own righteousness; flesh-centered concerns, therefore, undermine its influence in our lives. We try to keep the law, but we cannot, because of the flesh.

Second, the flesh is sinful and condemned (verse 3). Jesus as God-in-flesh, deity in a fully human body, subjected himself to sharing our universal human condemnation, even though he remained sinless in his own earthly life.

Third, the flesh leads to death (verses 5, 6). Jesus' death is the ultimate confirmation that the flesh—our self-life—is doomed apart from God's intervening mercy and grace. The flesh will ultimately profit you nothing, even if you feel you have the "right to be happy." It will always lead to spiritual death.

Fourth, the flesh is hostile to God (verse 7). Since humanity is living in revolt *against* God— our self opposed to the Spirit—it is an obvious contradiction to suppose that we could simultaneously accept his authority in our state of rebellion.

Fifth, the flesh cannot please God (verse 8). What pleases God is human responsiveness to divine regulations—not merely so that we will know "who is boss," but so that we can enjoy fellowship with our Creator and with each other. God is not happy about our alienation from him or about our antagonisms toward each other.

This self-life of ours, therefore, would seem to present an almost overwhelming problem for every Christian. "But," says Paul with great emphasis, in verse 9, "you are not in the flesh, you are in the Spirit, if the Spirit of God really dwells in you." Look at that sequence in reverse order to underscore God's marvelous solution to our dilemma: If the Spirit of God really dwells in you ... you are in the Spirit ... you are not in the flesh." The Spirit in us, and we in the Spirit; that is the answer to the problem of the flesh.

Since the Christian warfare is spiritual, God's fighting forces must be spiritual, not fleshly. That is the absolute pre-requisite for our mobilization.

2. *Potential Handicaps*

While the simple fact is clear enough—that we are in Christ when the Spirit of Christ is in us, and thus we are no longer "in the flesh" in the sense of being rebels against God, strict care must be taken to avoid drawing two wrong inferences that might make us unfit for God's service. Before discussing them, though, a brief survey is in order.

Concerning what it means to have freedom both from "the flesh," and from sin, by being "in Christ," I personally find no clearer teaching anywhere in the New Testament than in Romans 6. I believe it to be one of the greatest chapters in the whole Bible, and one which thousands of Christians throughout the world claim has made the most profound difference in their lives.

Like all spiritual truths, of course, these must be taught by the Holy Spirit. You may understand mentally—intellectually—what this passage is saying without really seeing it spiritually. I myself gave Bible studies on Romans 6 for a whole year before I began to see and apply the spiritual truths I was expressing. Looking back on my notes, I see that the truth was all there, but my spiritual eyes were not wide open to it.

Open eyes
When at last I came to "see" what I had been

preaching to others for some time, I found myself rather like that glorious Anglican clergyman of another generation, William Haslam, who was converted in his own pulpit by his own sermon! As he was preaching, suddenly he "saw it." At that moment, someone at the back of the church building stood up and shouted: "The parson's converted! The parson's converted!" They all stood up and started praising God that their parson was converted. Oh, for a good many more William Haslams today!

I would suggest that, before you read any further, you quietly ask the Holy Spirit to help you, to teach you, to speak to you, to encourage you according to your personal need. The Holy Spirit is the supreme teacher of God's Word, so ask him to give you spiritual understanding.

As to the exact interpretation of this passage in Romans 6, frankly there is some division of opinion among Bible scholars. Paul is talking here about freedom from sin—all will agree to that. Some would say, though, that he is speaking about freedom from the *penalty* of sin, while others hold that the *power* of sin is the issue.

On the shelves of my study, I have 22 commentaries on the Epistle to the Romans. I enjoy them and turn to most, if not all of them from time to time. Yet, on this particular interpretation, one can divide the 22 illustrious and scholarly commentators into two equal teams. It would be quite wrong, even presumptuous of me, to claim to be the referee and decide which side is the winner.

However, I find that for me, personally, the most convincing interpretation is one held by such expositors as Martyn Lloyd-Jones, John Murray, John Calvin, C. J. Vaughan, Griffith Thomas, F. Godet, Anders Nygren and others—a very persuasive team which, I think, is moving in the right direction: namely that Paul's primary focus here is on freedom from the *power* of sin.

Two fundamental realms

Look at the chapters leading up to Romans 6. In chapters 1-3, Paul spells out the *fact* of sin, that Jews and Gentiles alike have sinned and are guilty before God and are under God's judgment. At the end of Chapter 3, Paul asks how God can be both just and the justifier of the sinner at the same time. How can a sinner be forgiven and accepted by a holy God? There is only one answer: through faith in Jesus Christ and his blood. Then, in Chapter 4, Paul expands on the whole nature of the faith that saves. In Chapter 5 we come to the apex of the whole book of Romans, where Paul sets out both the parallel and the contrast between Adam, on the one hand, and Christ on the other. Here are two fundamental realms in which everyone lives. The diagram here may help us to grasp this more clearly.

On the left there is the kingdom of Satan, consisting of all those who are "in Adam." On the right, the kingdom of God includes all those who

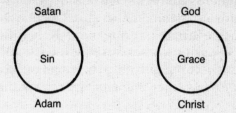

are "in Christ." In Adam we are under the penalty of sin, under the power of sin, bound by the law and subject to death. But in Christ we are set free from all these things, and in Romans 5, 6, 7 and 8 Paul spells out the Christian's freedom. We are free from the penalty of sin (chapter 5), free from the power of sin (chapter 6), free from bondage to law (chapter 7), and free from death (chapter 8), meaning spiritual death. Paul is convinced that absolutely nothing can separate us from the love of God in Christ Jesus.

Now we can see how the opening question in Chapter 6 fits in. In Chapter 5 Paul has been explaining the complete and absolute forgiveness of sin in Christ. "Therefore, since we are justified by faith, we have peace with God through our Lord Jesus Christ" (Romans 5:1); and in verse 20, "Law came in, to increase the trespass; but where sin increased, grace abounded all the more, so that, as sin reigned in death, grace also might reign through righteousness to eternal life through Jesus Christ our Lord." Therefore, in the diagram I have put SIN at the center of the kingdom of Satan because sin reigns in that realm. In the kingdom of God I have put GRACE because grace reigns in that realm. Now, the natural question following those verses, especially Romans 5:20, is in Romans 6:1, "What shall we say then? Are we to continue in sin that grace may abound?"

Comfortably complacent

This chapter, then, has special value for two sorts of people. It is written first of all for a Christian who has such assurance of forgiveness that he may be tempted to be a little careless with his own life and behavior. This can be a special snare in evangelical circles where we glory (and rightly so) in the finished work of Christ on the cross. Since I have put my trust in my Savior I am forgiven and cleansed from all my sin. I know that if I confess my sin God is faithful and just to forgive my sin. However, if I glory in this without grasping the implications of this magnificent truth, I could become lazy and undisciplined in my prayer and my Bible study. I might be apathetic when it comes to Christian service. I might become a little too casual in my relationships with the opposite sex. I might grow rather critical of others. I might be less than loving to those with whom I disagree. I might even forget God's holiness. I might grow indifferent to the needs and problems of other people.

I believe that many Christians, quite frankly, play with their Christianity and flirt with sin. But

Paul asks here, "Are we to continue in sin that grace may abound? He answers, "By no means! How can we who died to sin still live in it?" If anyone has a true understanding of the utter sinfulness of sin, that it ruins and spoils our lives; if anyone knows anything of the holiness of God who "is of purer eyes than to behold evil and cannot look on iniquity;" if anyone knows anything of the cross of Jesus Christ—then sin cannot be an accepted part of our lives. Someone has said this about sin, "It took the loveliest life in all the world (Christ's) and smashed it on a cross."

Let me ask you a very personal question, which I have often asked myself: *Are you, in any way, acting a lie in your Christian life?* If you are a Christian, you are "in Christ," and if you are "in Christ" you are "dead to sin and alive to God." But does any part of your life deny to that? In your home, in your relationships, in your work, in your time and money, does any part deny what you are in Christ? If so, two serious consequences follow: First, you are denying the Gospel by your life. You are saying, by your life, "Jesus does not save." Krishna, having watched the lives of Christians for many years, had to say this, "Christians claim that Jesus is their Savior, but they show no more signs of being saved than anyone else." Another Indian said, "I would become a Christian if I could see one."

The second damaging consequence is that you are despising the cross of Jesus Christ. Someone has said that sin is like slapping Christ in the face: "You died for me on the cross, you bore my sins —but I don't care." And the Bible has many warnings to the effect that if we continue in sin, having known Jesus Christ, we are crucifying the Son of God afresh and holding him up to contempt. Are you acting a lie? Then you are denying the Gospel and you are despising the cross.

Dangerously depressed

At the other extreme from the dangerously complacent Christians is the second group—the dangerously depressed ones. They are also grateful to have been saved from ultimate spiritual death and eternal separation from God, which is the penalty of sin. They regard their earthly experience in the meantime, however, as an apparently endless and usually futile struggle against sin, which seems to maintain the upper hand. They are ignorant of the liberating truth discussed by Paul in Romans 6.

These people may read the great promises in the New Testament about victory over sin, that "we are more than conquerors through him who loved us." They may sing vigorously that magnificient hymn by Charles Wesley: "He breaks the power of cancelled sin; he sets the prisoner free." But the feeling that it is not that way in their personal experience breeds an attitude of *defeat*. That, in turn, can lead to *deceit*—a pretense to themselves and others that all is well when, in fact, it is not. What quickly follows is *depression,* a mood of hopelessness and pessimism and disgust with self. There must be many Christians in that miserable state of mind, judging from the fact that Dr. Martyn Lloyd-Jones' book, *Spiritual Depression,* became a best-seller almost overnight!

Again, may I probe deeply with another personal question: *Are you in any way defeated in your Christian life?* Is there some persistent temptation which always seems to master you? Consider carefully, then, your freedom in Christ. Let the Holy Spirit convince you that you are dead to sin, alive to God. Let him lead you to the cross of Jesus Christ to confess that bondage to sin, to know his forgiveness and cleansing, and to help you claim the freedom which is yours in Christ, who has come to set you free from sin's bondage. Believe his Word, claim it, reflect on it, know it to be true, praise him for it. To the degree that you believe it and act upon it, it will become true in your experience. Then you will really begin to prove that Jesus does save, that his salvation brings true freedom. He *does* break the power of cancelled sin. He *does* set the prisoner free. It is that reality which the world is desperately waiting to see in our lives today.

To repeat—over-confident complacency or despairing depression: these are two dangers that will disqualify a Christian from waging the war on God's side against Satan, and winning it! Obviously such a state of affairs does not please the

Lord—but neither does it daunt nor discourage him! Through his servant Paul, the Holy Spirit reveals to us the divine solution.

3. Dead—but on Duty!

In Romans 6 we find both a fact to consider and an act to perform. To be qualified as soldiers in God's army, Christians must submit their minds to the discipline of truth and their wills to the exercise of God's sovereign authority.

A fact to consider. When God gives us something to think about, it is not abstract theory or idle speculation. Rather, it is truth, fact, reality. Repeatedly in this outstanding biblical passage Paul writes about "knowing" (verses 3, 6, 9). He deals with facts, not guesses. The most astonishing fact of all is presented in verse 11: "You must consider yourselves dead to sin and alive to God in Christ Jesus."

"Consider yourselves dead." Sounds preposterous, doesn't it? Is it telling us that Christians comprise a company of the walking dead? Hardly. They are, on the contrary, the most vital and alert beings in all creation because they are "alive to God," who is the very source of life. Yet their "death" is more than a figure of speech.

A vast difference exists between objective fact and subjective experience. Once there was a man who was quite convinced that he was dead. His friends tried to persuade him he was not, but their arguments didn't convince him. Eventually his psychiatrist said, "Well, I think there's one way I can convince him. I'll try to show him that dead men do not bleed." After being shown various medical textbooks, the poor man eventually said, "All right, I believe you. Dead men do not bleed." Whereupon the psychiatrist, with great confidence, picked up a scalpel and sliced into the man's arm, causing it to bleed freely. The patient, horrified at the sight, exclaimed, "Goodness me! Dead men do bleed after all!" Here was a man who *felt* he was dead. The facts made no impression at all on his strong feelings.

Now in this passage in Romans it is the other way round. Some people may *feel* that they are very much alive to sin; but Paul is saying, "No. *This* is a fact. You must know this. You must consider this—that you are dead to sin and alive to God (verse 11). I am told that the word "consider" in the Greek was used in the field of accounting. It means that you have to make a careful calculation. There must be no mistake. You *are* dead to sin and alive to God.

Further, what Paul has to say here applies to every single Christian: "Do you not know that *all* of us who have been baptized into Christ Jesus"— every single Christian believer, not just those who have had special experiences, but all of us—"were baptized into his death" (verse 3). In other words, when Christ died on the cross, not only did he die for us but we died in him. And in the Greek this word *died* is in the aorist tense. It means "once for all." Just as Christ died once for all, so we have died in Christ once for all. You can see how insistent Paul is about the fact of this death, because he stresses it in practically every verse of the first eleven. He is very emphatic about it.

R.S.V.P.

Two sisters, Mary and Jane Brown, were both converted the same day. The next day they were formally invited to some kind of party which they knew would be wild, and they felt that as newborn Christians they could not attend it. In their reply to the invitation they wrote: "Mary and Jane Brown thank you for your kind invitation but regret that they cannot attend. They died yesterday." That was good theology because now they were dead to sin and alive to God. Indeed, verse 2 might be more accurately translated: "Shall we continue in sin that grace may abound? By no means! How can *we, we* who died to sin, still live in it?" The emphasis is on the word "we." It is unthinkable that we should continue in sin. We're dead!

As a basis for understanding this astonishing fact, we must confront the foundational question: *How did we die to sin?* The answer, as we have seen already, is through the cross of Jesus Christ: "We know that our old self was crucified with him" (Romans 6:6). "If we have died with Christ, we believe that we shall also live with him" (verse 8). When Christ died and was buried, we died in him and were buried with him.

I have bridged the two realms with the cross, because that is the only possible way by which we can leave one realm and enter the other.

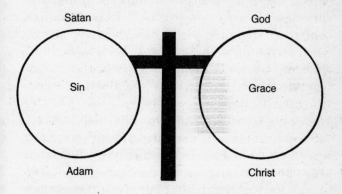

Further, all that happened for us at the cross was personally appropriated at the time of our baptism, or union with Christ: "Do you not know that all of us who have been baptized into Christ Jesus were baptized into his death? We were buried therefore with him by baptism into death" (Romans 6:3, 4).

Now some people get side-tracked at this point, and as soon as they see this word "baptism," they "immerse" themselves in the whole question of water baptism, infant or otherwise, sprinkling or otherwise—and the devil loves to get us all worked up over issues like this. Well, I'm not going to "plunge" into this subject, or even "dip" into it! Paul is not talking here about the outward rite, or its symbolism. What he is emphasizing is our union with Christ, as we can see clearly in verse 5, "For if we have been united with him in a death like his, we shall certainly be united with him in a resurrection like his." In other words, once we are united with Christ, we have already died with him, we have already been buried with him, we have already been raised with him and therefore *are now* dead to sin and alive to God. It's as real a fact as the cross itself.

Let me try to illustrate this still further, as it is so important to see this clearly. Imagine a refugee escaping from East Berlin into West Berlin. In East Berlin he has known the fear and bondage and misery of that realm; but at last the moment comes when he is able to escape from it and enter a different realm altogether—West Berlin, a free zone. He must cross that crucial frontier between the two realms, out of fear into freedom. From now on, the ruling authorities of East Berlin will no longer have any legal right to limit or direct his activities. They may shout warnings or threats over the wall at him but they cannot touch him. He is free, no longer bound by their authority.

Therefore, when Paul says, "We know that our old self was crucified with him so that the sinful body might be destroyed, and we might no longer be enslaved to sin" he is saying that the demands of sin should have no effect whatever on us. He is saying, "You *are* entirely delivered now from the rule and reign of sin. Don't be a slave to it, because you *aren't* a slave to it! Don't live as though you were in Adam. You *are not* in Adam." A father may perhaps tell his teenage son, "Don't be a baby!" The boy is not a baby, there's no question about that! No baby is six feet tall and beginning to grow a beard! What the father is really saying is, "Don't be a baby. Be your age. Be *what you are*." So it is with us in Christ. We must become what we really are. We are in Christ and sin has no dominion over us. Paul exhorts us to consider a fact, that we are "dead to sin and alive to God in Christ Jesus."

Marvelous as the fact is, that in Christ we died to sin's penalty and power, another important question still confronts us: What does it *mean* to be dead to sin? Every fact carries its implications; this particular fact produces astounding consequences in a Christian's life. It is urgent, therefore, to clarify any possible confusion caused by various interpretations of Paul's teaching here.

i) Some say it means "dead to the *influence* of sin," dead to temptation, the very desire of sin. This argument leads to the doctrine of Perfectionism. But that is obviously false. See Romans 6:12, where Paul enjoins us "let not sin therefore reign." If we are dead to the influence, why would he need to warn us? Why does he repeat his warning in verse 13, "Do not yield your members?" John says "If we say we have no sin, we deceive

ourselves, and the truth is not in us" (1 John 1:8).
At one conference a speaker was teaching some
form of sinless perfection. The other speaker,
Charles Spurgeon, said nothing at the time but the
next day at breakfast he poured a pitcher of milk
over the head of the other speaker, to test his doctrine, which was shown, quite definitely, to be false!

ii) Others say, "This means that we are *dying
daily to sin.*" Of course there is great truth in that;
but Paul here uses the aorist tense. He does not
say that we *are dying* or that we *must die* but that we
are *already dead*. We died, once for all.

iii) Many take this to mean that we are dead to
the *guilt* of sin, and that is perfectly and wonderfully true. But I believe there is something even
more than that here.

iv) This is the Gospel of Freedom from *all* the
consequences of sin including its power and
bondage; and some day, freedom from its very
presence, when we are with the Lord in heaven
for eternity. Further, Paul clearly has this idea of
power and bondage very much in mind, for at the
end of verse 6 of Romans 6 he says that "we might
no longer be *enslaved* to sin," and again in verse
14, "Sin will have no *dominion* over you, since you
are not under the law but under grace." We must
constantly keep in mind the two realms (see diagram on page 49).

A new realm
Paul says, in chapter 5, that in the realm of Adam,

sin reigned. But the Christian has now died to the reign of sin from the moment of his justification. Now he has left that realm and entered the realm of freedom; now he is in the kingdom of God; now he is in Christ; now grace reigns in his life. The conclusion is that now he is wonderfully free from this reign of sin. As Paul says in chapter 6, verse 7, "he who has died is freed from sin;" and in so far as we consider this as a fact and live in the light of it, then it will become increasingly real in our personal lives. Then we can truly say we have already died, we are already free.

However, although it is a simple fact that we are now free, we may not immediately experience the full reality of that freedom. We may still have nightmares, we may still have sudden fears, we may still live as though we were in the old realm. But as we begin to consider ourselves dead to the old realm and alive to the new realm, then steadily and increasingly we will experience this freedom.

"Let not sin therefore reign in your mortal bodies, to make you obey their passions" (verse 12). How ridiculous it would be to say those words to a non-Christian, for he is in Adam where sin does reign. He cannot help his bondage. But it makes a lot of sense to say "Let not. . . ." to a child of God because now he is in Christ where sin does not reign. Paul is saying, "Don't live as though you were in that old realm."

Slavery, shame, separation
When a Christian sins, he sins as a free man who

is choosing to do wrong, or as a free man who does not yet appreciate his freedom. Dr. Martyn Lloyd-Jones once put it in this striking form: "The Christian who sins is a fool!" You see, sin is a thoroughly wretched and miserable thing. From this chapter it is evident, first of all in verse 16, that sin leads to *slavery*. "Do you not know that if you yield yourselves to anyone as obedient slaves, you are slaves of the one whom you obey, either of sin, which leads to death, or of obedience, which leads to righteousness?" Jesus once said, "Whoever commits sin is the slave of sin." Second, sin leads to *shame*: "But then what return did you get from the things of which you are now ashamed?" (verse 21). There is not a single Christian who can knowingly do something wrong in God's sight who is not ashamed of it afterward. Third, sin leads to *separation*. "The end of those things is death" (verse 21)—death meaning separation from God and true life.

Therefore the Christian who sins is a miserable Christian. He has been robbed of the joy and peace that he ought to experience in Jesus Christ. Remember how King David, when he committed that double sin of adultery and murder, inwardly suffered absolute misery for a whole year, though outwardly all seemed well. Read Psalm 32, which he wrote later, after his initial confession of sin (Psalm 51) and you will see this. He looks back on the situation, remembering that for a whole year he did not confess his sin. He says this, "Blessed is the man to whom the Lord imputes no iniquity, and in whose spirit there is no deceit. When I declared not my sin, my body wasted away through my groaning all day long. For day and night thy hand was heavy upon me; my strength was dried up as by the heat of summer . . . Many are the pangs of the wicked; but steadfast love surrounds him who trusts in the Lord."

I remember vividly a time when for some weeks and months I was seriously disobeying the Lord. Every time I went to church it was an agonizing experience, because the preacher seemed to know all about me and to say all he knew! And the Word of God went through me again and again. "Many are the pangs of the wicked!" Indeed, wherever there is something in our lives which is displeasing to God (and we know it) we are in a miserable state. And because God loves us, that misery and unhappiness will increase until we get right with him. Sin leads to slavery, shame and separation. The obvious question is, "Why live in it, then?" The Christian who sins is a fool!

More than that, he is despising what Christ has done for him on the cross to bring him freedom. Therefore Paul says in Romans 6:13, "Do not yield your members to sin as instruments of wickedness, but yield yourselves to God as men who have been brought from death to life, and your members to God as instruments of righteousness." You are not in Satan's realm now. You are in

God's realm through the cross of Jesus Christ. Are you forgetting, or even despising that reality?

Free to fight

Dr. Martyn Lloyd-Jones once said that Christianity is far too often presented as a remedy for all our problems—"Come to the clinic and we'll give you all the loving care and attention that you need to help you with your problems." But, comments Dr. Lloyd-Jones,

> in the Bible I find a barracks, not a hospital. It is not a doctor you need but a drill sergeant. Here we are on the parade ground slouching around. A doctor won't help us. It is discipline we need. We need to listen to our Sergeant. "Yield not to temptation but yield yourselves to God." This is the trouble with the Church today; there is too much of the hospital element; they have lost sight of the great battle.[2]

And if you are involved with a great battle there is only one thing that counts—your Leader and your country. Your own personal needs and problems are relatively unimportant. So it is when we are engaged in this tremendous warfare in the spirit, serving as soldiers of Jesus Christ. We need this element of discipline in the warfare. We are free indeed—*free to fight!* Therefore, "Let not sin reign . . . Do not yield your members as instruments of wickedness."

Christians are free! Through the atoning death of the Lord Jesus Christ, they have been liberated from death, which is the penalty for their sins. They have been transferred from the fatal realm of the flesh to the vital realm of the spirit. This qualifies them to join with the Lord God Almighty in the battle he is waging in this world against Satan and sin. They have been freed *from* death's penalty and power, and freed *for* frontline duty in winning the war and reclaiming the world for Christ. They are commissioned to act with God's authority backing them.

Satan knows all of that, of course, and is utterly determined not to give an inch of ground without a struggle. Next, therefore, we must examine the Enemy.

Notes

[1]Leon Morris, *The Spirit of the Living God,* (Great Britain: Inter-Varsity Press).
[2]Martyn Lloyd-Jones, *Spiritual Depression: It's Causes and Cure,* (Great Britain: Pickering and Inglis).

Enemy Strategy

3

"Your adversary the devil prowls around like a roaring lion..." *(I Peter 5:8).*

Every army has its "intelligence unit" with responsibility to secure all the information it can about the enemy: his strength, equipment, tactics and above all, his strategy—the plan he has for the battle. Naturally, the enemy wants to keep all of this "classified," a secret, and will try anything to deceive and mislead us.

The enemy of our souls, Satan, is driven to destroy us by one malicious motive—he wants to thwart God's purpose for us and thus cheat God of glory due to him. He doesn't take kindly to any investigation of his methods.

As a result, this discussion can be highly dangerous. Might it not be better, and surely much safer, to concentrate on Jesus and give Satan the silent treatment?

C. S. Lewis has given a clear warning about this: "There are two equal and opposite errors into which our race can fall about the devils. One is to disbelieve in their existence. The other is to believe, and to feel an excessive and unhealthy interest in them. They themselves are equally pleased by both errors and hail a materialist or a magician with the same delight."[1]

We are in trouble if we pay no attention to Satan, and we are in trouble if we pay him too much attention. Let us base our study, therefore, on Scripture, praying all the while that the Holy Spirit will be our Guide and Protector.

1. Four Biblical Reasons for Investigating Satan.

A. The Bible makes many references to Satan and his works. If we are to study the "whole counsel of God," we cannot afford to ignore these unpopular truths, such as the 35 or more references to occultism alone. (For further study, note the passages mentioned at the end of this chapter.)

B. There is an urgent practical reason for not being ignorant about these things. In 2 Corinthians 2:10, 11 Paul explains that the reason for a certain action is "to keep Satan from gaining the advantage over us; for we are not ignorant of his designs." Any ignorance on our part gives Satan added leverage over us.

C. We are commanded to test the spirits, as John says (1 John 4:1-3):

> Beloved, do not believe every spirit, but test the spirits to see whether they are of God; for many false prophets have gone out into the world. By this you know the Spirit of God: every spirit which confesses that Jesus

Christ has come in the flesh is of God, and every spirit which does not confess Jesus is not of God. This is the spirit of antichrist, of which you heard that it was coming, and now it is in the world already.

How can we test the spirits unless we know something about them and know what this test is?

D. We are commissioned to wage war against the powers of darkness. Jesus said to the seventy he sent out (Luke 10:19): "I have given you authority to tread on serpents and scorpions, and over all the power of the enemy." In Ephesians 6, Paul gives detailed instruction about this warfare, reminding us that "we are not contending against flesh and blood, but against the principalities, against the powers, against the world rulers of this present darkness, against the spiritual hosts of wickedness in the heavenly places."

I believe, therefore, that we must study the devil and all his works, potentially dangerous as such a study may be. Remember that we have two indispensable and invincible safeguards: The first is that *we start from and stay with the Bible* and the second that *we trust personally in the name and in the blood of Jesus Christ.*

2. The Enemy's Nature

We are not told very much about Satan's origin except that he is a fallen angel thrown out of heaven because of the sin of pride (Isaiah 14: 12-14):

How are you fallen from heaven, O Day Star, son of Dawn! How you are cut down to the ground, you who laid the nations low! You said in your heart, "I will ascend into heaven; above the stars of God I will set my throne on high; I will sit on the mount of assembly in the far north; I will ascend above the heights of the clouds; I will make myself like the Most High."

Notice two things from this passage. First—Satan's name: he is called here "Day Star, son of Dawn." I think that says that he is not a grotesque monster with horns and hooves and trident fork. Originally he was called (in Ezekiel 28) "perfect in beauty," and can therefore easily masquerade as an angel of light. Second—notice his ambition: "I will make myself like the Most High." This, of course, is the temptation he presents to Adam and Eve, "When you eat of this fruit," he says, "you will be *like God*." It was because of his pride and ambition that Satan and his angel-followers were condemned and thrown out of heaven. The consequence of that fall is that Satan and his angels lost their heavenly bodies and are therefore, now, disembodied spirits, who are "seeking rest," as Jesus describes it in Luke 11. That is why there is such a phenomenon as demon possession. One or more body-less evil spirits will come to occupy a human body (or a house or an animal) because they are seeking a place to stay—a material entity to control for their own purposes.

The word "Satan" is the Hebrew word for *adversary*; and this is the most significant characteristic of Satan. Peter calls him "your adversary, the devil." Notice that he is primarily the adversary of God, not of people. The whole world lies in the arms of the evil one, and provided you are unaware, asleep, in Satan's arms, he is not particularly bothered with you and you may not be bothered much by him. You belong in his kingdom anyway. He will not give you any permanent joy or satisfaction because he is ultimately leading you to destruction and robbing you of the eternal riches of Jesus Christ, and his wages are death. But he is not primarily *your* adversary.

But when you become a Christian and turn from darkness to light, from the dominion of Satan to the kingdom of God, then he actively comes against you because he is against God and anything belonging to God. And the more you are used by God, the more you are filled by his Spirit, the more Satan will attack you. This has been my constant experience—particularly when leading an evangelistic outreach. Often these attacks will involve members of my family.

Corrie ten Boom once said, when she began to teach Christians about spiritual warfare, "Whenever I gave this message, I was so tired I could hardly reach my bed. My heart beat irregularly and I felt ill."[2] She was tempted to drop this subject altogether and talk about something entirely different. When she realized that Satan was trying to undermine her strength and her confidence in the Lord, she claimed the victory in the name of Jesus and regained his peace.

So, we understand from God's Word that our enemy is "angelic" in his origin and may be compellingly attractive, but also that he is proudly ambitious which makes him the adversary of God and all who are on God's side.

3. The Enemy's Disguises

Satan is exceedingly shrewd and cunning. He knows that if he were to attack us with a full display of his hideous, warped hatred of God, we would recoil and have nothing to do with him. He has to resort to tricks and comes to us in many different roles, wearing a variety of masks intended to fool or impress us.

A. *The Invisible Man.* In this guise, Satan pretends he does not exist and many people have believed this lie. That is why the "enlightened" churches of today, which do not believe in the existence of the Devil, are so often lifeless and powerless. They are truly under his power but fail to realize it. McNeile Dixon once wrote,

The kindhearted humanitarians of the nineteenth century decided to improve on Christianity. The thought of Hell offended their susceptibilities. They closed it, and to their surprise the gates of Heaven closed also, with a melancholy bang. The malignant countenance of Satan disturbed them. They dispensed with him and at the same time God took His departure.[3]

As another writer put it:

"The devil was fairly voted out,
And of course, the devil's gone.
But simple folk would like to know
Who carries his business on!"

B. The Angel of Light. In 2 Corinthians 11:13-15 Paul writes about false teachers: "Such men are false apostles, deceitful workmen, disguising themselves as apostles of Christ. And no wonder, for even Satan disguises himself as an angel of light. So it is not strange if his servants also disguise themselves as servants of righteousness. Their end will correspond to their deed."

Satan may use certain messengers who appear to be ministers of Christ to teach new and intriguing interpretations of Scripture. Or they may claim some special and unusual revelation from God, which goes beyond God's Word. Often they will show a subtle and mystical form of super-spirituality, as is particularly evident in many of the currents sects and cults. Mary Baker Eddy wrote these words about her Christian Science textbook, *Science and Health:*

It was not myself, but the divine power of truth and love infinitely above me, which dictated *Science and Health.* I should blush to write this book, as I have, were it of human origin and I apart from God its author; but as I was only a scribe, echoing the harmonies of heaven in divine metaphysics, I cannot be supermodest in my estimation of the Christian Science textbook.[4]

To the unwary this may sound very disarming, but it is of the utmost presumption for her to claim that her book has been inspired by God. One further point to remember: the "angel of light" can easily quote Scripture out of context, to his own advantage, and does so freely.

C. The Father of Lies. Jesus says in the passage beginning with John 8:43,

Why do you not understand what I say? It is because you cannot bear to hear my Word. You are of your father the devil, and your will is to do your father's desires. He was a murderer from the beginning, and has nothing to do with the truth, because there is no truth in him. When he lies, he speaks according to his own nature, for he is a liar and the father of lies.

Strong words! The great lie that he deceives us with again and again is that he promises great rewards, as he did to Jesus in the wilderness temptation: "To you," he said as he showed Christ all the kingdoms of the world, "I will give all this authority and their glory if you, then, will worship me." Today he may tell us, "I'll give you an easy life; I'll allow you success; I'll grant you happiness; I'll reward you with wealth and prestige." But remember Jesus' words, 'What does it profit a man to gain the whole world and forfeit his life?"

Again, he may tempt us to be super-spiritual. A Christian, for example, may refuse all medical help because "the Lord alone is my doctor." Now, I believe that the Lord *is* the great Physician and I have no doubt that we *should* look to the Lord much more than we do for physical and mental and emotional needs as well as spiritual ones. But while it is true that the Lord can and does heal today, truth that is exaggerated becomes error. Heresy, means, literally, going off on a tangent. If we take a point of truth within the balanced circle of teaching in the Scripture and take it out of balance, off on a tangent by itself, it becomes an exaggeration and therefore a departure from the truth as given by God. Satan knows all about those errors, those tangents. He is the father of them!

Another common tactic of Satan's is to spread false gossip and rumor about other Christians. This can cause destructive damage to God's work and divide his children so that their energies are expended in opposing each other instead of withstanding their common foe and winning their way to freedom in Christ.

D. The Serpent. Satan beguiles us and entices us into sin. When it comes to God's Word it is very important that we stick to the truth, the whole truth and nothing but the truth. We must neither change it, nor subtract from it, nor add to it. In the temptation of Adam and Eve we find that the Serpent there does all those three things with God's Word and thereby seeks to undermine it. "Did God say? Has God said? Are you really sure?"

We see the same temptation at the start of Jesus' ministry when he was baptized. There God the Father said, "You are my beloved Son." The moment he was in the wilderness the Tempter spoke to him twice, introducing an element of doubt; *"If* you are the Son of God. . . . *If* you are the Son of God." He may say to us, likewise, *"If* you are a Christian believer, why do you behave like this? Why don't you *feel* more of the reality of God? *If* Jesus is with you, why don't you know more of his power in your daily experience? *If* you are really dead to sin and alive to God, why are you so selfish?" If. If. If. The Serpent!

E. The Accuser. John writes, in Revelation 12:10, "The accuser of our brethren . . . who accuses them day and night." The very word "devil" means accuser or slanderer, the emphasis being on the falsity of the accusation. He may accuse you like this: "You're such a failure, such a miserable Christian. Look at all your sins. Look at your selfishness. How can God love you or even *use* you? You're too much of a problem to him." Or again, Satan may accuse you by introducing some doubt that you are in the place of God's choosing; "You've mistaken God's guidance. You're in a place where God cannot use you." He gets you all confused and frustrated, wondering where you made such a desperate mistake.

Of course we may all make mistakes about guidance, but as we surrender our possible mistakes to the Lord, he can take them and even use them for his glory. But the devil goes on nagging, nagging, nagging—trying to rob us of our peace in the Lord Jesus.

Notice his methods. Sometimes he creeps up behind us, whispering some blasphemous thought in our ear. Then, before we realize what has happened, he whips around in front of us and says "You call yourself a Christian? With a thought like *that* in your mind?" Have you known, during times of prayer, the most impure, lustful thoughts attacking you? Well, that is Satan, the accuser, putting thoughts in your mind and then accusing you for having them there.

F. The Roaring Lion. This name applies during a particularly powerful attack, perhaps of fear, guilt, sickness, depression or persecution. Peter tells his readers to "be sober, be watchful. Your adversary the devil prowls around like a roaring lion, seeking someone to devour. Resist him, firm in your faith, knowing the same experience of suffering is required of your brotherhood throughout the world."

G. *The Prince of the Power of the Air*. As a prince, Satan has a great legion of evil spirits working for him. He is the prince of this world and the New Testament speaks of such spirits as the spirit of error, an unclean spirit (usually a spirit of lust), a seducing spirit (suggesting the unbalanced view of some truth), a deaf spirit, a dumb spirit, a spirit of fear, a lying spirit (giving false guidance or false prophecy), and a familiar spirit (manifesting itself through a medium). All these are utterly evil and opposed to God.

Since Satan can employ so many clever disguises, we can see how critical it is for us to "test the spirits." The enemy must be unmasked so that his true character becomes evident to everyone.

4. The Enemy's Tactics

The enemy is both powerful and intelligent; and unless we understand this we shall be defeated, depressed, harassed and ineffective. "We are not contending against flesh and blood, but against the principalities, against the powers . . ." (Ephesians 6:12). There are three main forms of satanic attack as seen from this passage:

A. *Subtlety*. "Put on the whole armor of God, that you may be able to stand agains the *wiles* of the devil" (verse 11). In the last section we looked at his wiles in terms of his being an angel of light, the father of lies, the Serpent, etc. Therefore, in Ephesians 4 Paul urges his readers to go on "to mature manhood, to the measure of the stature of the fulness of Christ; so that we may no longer be children, tossed to and fro and carried about with every wind of doctrine, by the cunning of men, by their craftiness in deceitful wiles." Never under-estimate the subtlety of the enemy. The New Testament epistles were written simply because in those early days the Christians were so often deceived by the devil and Paul had to write careful, detailed instructions for them, saying, in effect, "Now don't be children, unsure of yourselves, believing now one thing, now another. Be mature. Be strong. Understand the devil's tactics so that he cannot attack and overcome you!"

B. Siege. "Therefore take the whole armor of God, that you may be able to withstand in the evil day" (verse 13). This, I believe, refers to a serious and sometimes prolonged assault of the evil one, perhaps through a time of severe illness, or an accident which for the moment knocks you right out of the battle. Or it may be a time of continuing dark depression.

A few years ago I had a very serious illness. There were many nights in which I could hardly sleep at all. Frequently, during those long night hours, I read and re-read the Psalms. They seemed to speak so vividly of my own experience. One of my favorite Psalms at that time was Psalm 13 in which the psalmist says, "How long, O Lord?

Wilt thou forget me forever? How long wilt thou hide thy face from me? How long must I bear pain in my soul, and have sorrow in my heart all the day? How long shall my enemy be exalted over me?" How long? How long? How long? "Consider and answer me, O Lord my God; lighten my eyes, lest I sleep the sleep of death." Many Christians experience this seige from Satan, and cry out in their hearts, "How long, O Lord? How long? How long?"

James Philip wrote at the beginning of his commentary on Christian warfare, "The preaching of this passage (Ephesians 6:10 ff) became very real and came to mean a great deal to me when I was passing through a time of fierce and prolonged testing when all the powers of darkness seemed to be let loose on my soul and were intent, so it seemed, on bringing me crashing down; and it was in these days that God revealed to me two things: the richness and completeness of our position in Christ and what He has made us in Him, and the divine provision in the armour of light against all the assaults of the enemy. In those days morning prayer for me was a matter of poring over this passage in urgent desperation, seeking to put on this divine armour piece by piece, to preserve me against the assaults of the devil that were sure to come before the day was very far advanced."[5]

C. Surprise. Satan, for all his disguises and tactics, would not be as formidable a foe to God's people if he would signal in advance what he is planning to do. But he is far too crafty and experienced in battle strategy to do anything so stupid as that. One of his most effective maneuvers is to take us completely by surprise, catching us unexpectedly when we are off guard.

In Ephesians 6:16, Paul talks about the "flaming darts of the evil one." A dart is noiseless and swift, especially the type that is expelled from a blow-gun by hunters in certain primitive societies. Without warning, its sudden sting pierces its target and spreads it lethal poison.

All too often, Satan has been able to do some of his most destructive work in Christian's lives while they are experiencing the glow of some spiritual success, some heightened awareness of God. Perhaps it was the inspiration of a powerful sermon, or a special insight gained in a time of rich meditation on the Scriptures that lulled the believer into a less-than-alert attitude. Just at that point, Satan swiftly hurled a flaming dart that found its mark where he was unprotected and unsuspecting. The agony was intensified by the shock to his spirits. It may even have caused him to doubt the validity of the spiritual experience which he had just enjoyed.

Remember Paul's caution to us (1 Corinthians 10:12): "Therefore let anyone who thinks that he stands take heed lest he fall." Satan attacks without warning, and when we least expect it.

With such demonic skills at his disposal, the

enemy is not one to trifle with. It is inappropriate, to say the least, and downright foolhardy at the most, to make jokes about the devil. He is deadly serious in his war against God.

5. *The Enemy's Weapons*

With his customary diabolical cunning, Satan has fashioned implements of war that wreck infinitely greater devastation than any terrifying nuclear device. In our own day, I believe three of his most effective weapons demand our thoughtful analysis.

A. Cults. By cults I am referring, of course, not to other religions such as Buddhism, but to Christian Science, Mormonism, Unitarianism, the Jehovah's Witnesses, Christadelphianism, Theosophy, Scientology, Spiritualism, the Unification Church, the Children of God, and so on. The dictionary definition of a cult is this: "It is a devotion to a particular person or thing as paid by a body of professed adherents;" and that is a good definition because nearly all the cults follow a human leader as well as a set of doctrines.

Cults have three main characteristics. First, many of them seem, on the surface, to be *similar to true Christianity*. That is why they have deceived so many. I remember looking at some Mormon literature, and as I examined their beautifully designed, glossy magazine, I read page after page without discerning anything that was obviously unbiblical. It spoke reverently of God, about

Jesus, about the Spirit of God. It quoted the Bible. What was wrong with it? It was most deceptive because it looked so orthodox. The real points of difference with Bible theology were not displayed. They were hidden because they were rarely mentioned.

Second, cults usually offer *wonderful helps and blessings,* often far greater than we expect to find in more orthodox expressions of religion. The natural reaction of some people is, "Why haven't we heard about this before? This is exactly what we need!" Often cults flourish in times of stress and danger, perhaps during a national crisis. Just after the last World War, spiritualism made great advances because of the many thousands who had been killed in the war, whose relatives desperately attempted to regain contact with them. Cults offer special benefits for whose who are sick or sad or anxious. They may concentrate on prophecies about the Last Days—a subject of growing interest because of anxiety about world crises.

Third, cultic adherents are nearly always *sincere and zealous.* They are quite clear about what they believe and quite convinced of the truth of it. I have often asked Jehovah's Witnesses, "Why did you join this group?" So often the story is the same: "I was longing to know God. My local minister wasn't able to help me much. Then someone knocked on my door who seemed to have all the answers. He was so sure and so convinced about what he believed that I listened and accepted his message." Not unnaturally, the cults are enjoying some success today at a time when the established churches are discussing, *ad nauseum,* what they do *not* believe.

Five objective tests of the cults.

i) The *origin* of the cult. True Christianity depends entirely on the person of Jesus Christ. Because Christ *was* and *is* the son of God, what he said and did is of supreme importance. But most of the cults are based on various leaders whose personal lives, by any standard, leave much to be desired. That is why Christ said, in the Sermon on the Mount, "Beware of false prophets. . . . You will know them by their fruits." Take, for example, Jehovah's Witnesses. Their founder was C. T. Russell, a man who appeared in several courts of law on charges of shady financial dealings and in divorce proceedings. His successor was Judge Rutherford who was not a judge and was himself jailed for sedition.

ii) The *authority* of the cult. In any cult, some special authority—the Book of Mormon, for example—will be appealed to. And even if reference is made to the Bible, the main authority is always something other than the Bible. For example, Ron L. Hubbard, the guru of the Scientologists, says: "Thousands of philosophers have sought, every one of them from Socrates to Russell, the way to salvage the individual and society.

All right—we have found the way!" And if the "special knowledge" available through Scientology appeals to you, you will need, as basic equipment, a Ron L. Hubbard Mark V. Electrometer (retailing for at least £25), and then you will have only just started!

iii) The *essential doctrines* of the cults. By these doctrines I mean, to begin with, their views on the *person of Jesus Christ.* This is the ultimate test—"By this you know the Spirit of God: every spirit which confesses that Jesus Christ has come in the flesh is of God." Without expounding this in detail, it is enough to comment that John is showing how essential it is to believe that Jesus is both human and divine, both perfect man and perfect God. Unless Jesus is both human and divine there could be no Savior, no Mediator between man and God. Therefore, in the person of Jesus Christ, his humanity and his divinity together are essential. But you will not find that to be true in the cults. They may teach that Jesus was a great medium, or a great leader, or a great prophet or teacher, but they will never allow his divinity *and* his humanity.

Or again, with reference to the doctrine of the *Trinity,* most cults are unitarian and speak of God in terms of a "life force," an "eternal consciousness," and so on, usually with little reference to Jesus Christ or differentiation between God the Father and God the Spirit. Or, look carefully at their treatment of the doctrine of sin and the atonement and the need for repentance. Almost always these are entirely missing. Positive Thinking says this, "Believe in yourself. You're wonderful, if only you can realize it!" To them, the concept of sin is an insult. It is mere psychological inadequacy. Now if you really believe that, there is no need of Christ, there is no need for the Cross, or salvation or the new birth or repentance. Judgment is gone, hell is gone and heaven is gone with it.

iv) The *method* of the cult. Usually there is a simple formula or technique for "blessing." Recently, I studied carefully the Moral Re-Armament textbook titled *Remaking Men*. There is no reference in it to Christ except once where his name is quoted in the verse of a hymn. There are just four absolutes—Absolute honesty, purity, unselfishness and love. That is the secret of it all. Follow the four absolutes. In any cult the formula or the technique replaces a living relationship with Jesus Christ.

v) The *focus* of the cult. A Scientology advertisement calls you to "Free yourself from the barrier that holds *you* back in life. Let the real *you* emerge." God forbid! Dr. Martyn Lloyd-Jones comments on the man-centeredness of cults like this (the italics are mine): "It always starts with *you*. It comes to *you* and tells *you* that it can do this, that and the other for *you*. What do *you* need? What is *your* trouble? What is the matter with *you*? What are *you* looking for? Are *you* worried or troubled? Do *you* find it difficult to sleep? Are *you* over-anxious? Are *you* looking for peace? Are *you* looking for guidance?"[6] By contrast, Christianity starts with God: "In the beginning, God;" "God so loved the world." God, right at the very center, from the very beginning.

B. Occultism. It may be helpful to follow the divisions of this satanic weapon as suggested by Dr. Kurt Koch in his book *Occult Bondage and Deliverance.*[7]

First, is fortune-telling, such as astrology, palmistry, clairvoyance, etc. According to one fairly recent opinion poll, more than two-thirds of Britain's adults read their horoscopes, and about one fifth, or seven million, take them seriously. Over a third of the adult population believes in fortune telling. Sometimes, of course, it is manifestly a fake. On the very first day of a postal strike, when not a single letter was being delivered, one of the horoscopes in the daily papers said, "You will receive a letter today of considerable importance!"

Nevertheless, there have been some brilliant predictions. Perhaps the most famous of all was on November 22, 1963, when Jeane Dixon told her friends in Washington, D.C. "My mind isn't at ease today. I am afraid something terrible is about to happen." Shortly after that, the news was flashed throughout the whole world that President Kennedy had been assassinated. Since then, Jeane Dixon has become perhaps the best known fortune teller in North America. She has made a number of remarkable predictions and her books sell very widely. Though there is controversy about her, I believe that her predictions are supernatural messages from the Enemy.

Indeed, a marked rise in astrological foretelling is evident at the moment with the frequent publication of books with titles like: "Astrology Made Easy," "Astrology for Every Day," "The Astrological Guide to Health and Diet," "Astrology and Your Sex Life."

Next is magic, both black and white. Of course, those distinctions are deceptive. All magic is black and evil in God's sight. By "magic" I am referring either to the supernatural healing or inflicting of diseases, and to charms, curses, spells and the like. Examples of such practicioners in the New Testament would be Simon Magus and Elymas the Sorcerer. Magic is just as real and very common today.

Let me give you just one example. One man felt called to the Anglican ministry and went to a theological college in England. He was married, with children, and had been working in West Africa. During his theology course he became deeply depressed, so much so, even after psychiatric treatment, that the Principal of his college felt he could not possibly be ordained. However, at the Principal's suggestion, he went to see some Christian friends of mine. Together they prayed that God would reveal to one of them the basic cause of this depression. And it was in prayer that the man himself saw a vision. He saw that his African servant, who had been fired after some petty thievery, had gone to the local witch doctor and had had a curse put on him. Having seen this in the vision, the man returned to his praying friends and together they claimed the victory of Jesus and his blood. Today that man is normal, healthy and active in the ministry of the Gospel of Jesus Christ.

Third is spiritism. It involves such phenomena as table lifting, automatic writing, speaking in a trance and other forms of spirit communication, or what the Bible calls necromancy. Spiritualism is the name of the religion which practices spiritism. Recently the sale of ouija boards and other party games which call upon spirits to participate has risen steadily. So common is spiritism today that in Paris, according to *Time* magazine, there is one priest for every 5,000 people, one doctor for every 514, and one spiritualist for every 120.

What can we say about occultism in general? First of all, it is *devilish*. One of the passages of Scripture which deals specifically with this is Deuteronomy 18:9-14. There God says,

> When you come into this land which the Lord your God gives you, you shall not learn to follow the abominable practices of those nations. There shall not be found among you any one who burns his son or his daugh-

ter as an offering, any one who practices divination, a soothsayer, or an augur, or a sorcerer, or a charmer, or a medium, or a wizard or a necromancer. For whoever does these things is an abomination to the Lord; and because of these abominable practices the Lord your God is driving them out before you.

At a seance a spirit speaking through a medium was asked, "Do you believe in the devil?" The answer immediately came back, "Indeed we do. He is our god and father!" That is why all forms of spiritism are expressly condemned and forbidden in Scripture.

Not only is occultism devilish, it is *degrading*. Isaiah 8:19-20 tells us, "And when they say to you, 'Consult the mediums and the wizards who chirp and mutter,' should not a people consult their God? Should they consult the dead on behalf of the living? To the teaching and to the testimony (the Scriptures)! Surely for this word which they speak (these mediums and wizards who chirp and mutter), there is no dawn" (no light of truth to shine). When we have God's pure and powerful Word and his supreme revelation in his son Jesus Christ, and when we have all that we need to know about our present and our future, as well as about our past, to turn to mediums and wizards is to turn to the cheap, the false, the perverted. It is utterly degrading.

Occultism is also *deceptive*. Jesus warned his disciples in Matthew 24:24, "False Christs and false prophets will arise and show great signs and wonders, so as to lead astray, if possible, even the elect" (2 Thessalonians 2:9 and following verses). A woman pastor I know once told me of a couple who had begun to attend her church regularly. She asked them if they would like to consider becoming members of the church and they replied, "We'd like to, yes. But we are not quite sure if you would be entirely happy if we told you all about ourselves. We must be honest—the last five years our life has been wonderfully guided by an ouija board. It has directed our business life, told us about the house we should buy and it even told us to come to your church." (That last point was a masterly stroke of deception!) They went on to say how much they had prospered since they started consulting their ouija board for everything. The wise pastor said nothing. She knew the depth of their deception and she spent two days in prayer and fasting for them, praying the spirit behind this thing would reveal itself. She went back to their house after the two days. It had always been one of those homes which is always immaculately tidy, with everything in its place. But when she entered the front door it was as though a tornado had swept through that house. It was in absolute chaos and the couple themselves were distraught. The spirit in their lives had revealed itself in all its destructive, disordered reality. The devil and his followers are deceivers, from the beginning.

Occultism is also *damaging*. One of the leading spiritists in North America has said he does not know of a single case of a spiritist who has pursued the practice on a long term basis without displaying distinct deterioration of physical, mental or spiritual faculties. And that is the testimony of a spiritist! It *is* damaging. Dr. Koch mentions one fascinating point in his book *Occult Bondage and Deliverance*. "For years," he says, "I have witnessed the truth of the fact that magic and almost all other occult practices either destroy the Christian faith of a person or just prevent it from developing. And yet one finds that there is no conflict between sorcery and all the other world religions."[8] Here again the uniqueness of the Christian faith is demonstrated. Other religions can naturally embrace occultism. Only Christianity shows up the tremendous clash between the powers of darkness and the powers of light—for Christianity alone is the truth.

Occultism is damaging not only spiritually but also *mentally*. I think of one very fine, mature Christian girl in our own congregation. About a year ago she came under a suicidal depression. On three occasions she was right on the brink of committing suicide. She was counselled by doctors and by Christian workers. I myself talked and prayed with her. Still, she was utterly depressed, unable to concentrate on any work and sleeping unnaturally long hours. A friend brought her to one of our half nights of prayer, and there the whole local body of Christ gathered round her, praying earnestly, claiming victory over her depression in the name of Jesus. We were given a strong and lively confidence in the risen and powerful Lord. And she was instantly and completely delivered from her depression. She then wrote a long letter to me, describing some events which she had not been able to express before.

She came from a broken home and her mother was an active spiritualist. This girl was always rather fearful of seeing her mother, and Christians had been praying for her about it. When she went home, however, her mother described her occult activities until the small hours of the morning and uttered two satanic prophecies in the girl's presence. Immediately an awful oppression and darkness descended on the girl and she became deeply depressed. Occultism is definitely mentally damaging.

Occultism is also *physically* damaging and there are cases of paralysis, deafness, dumbness and other physical maladies resulting from occult involvement. Beware of the devil and all his works! Never play with these dark powers. I would also strongly advise Christians not to attempt to deliver a person oppressed by satanic power unless they know what they are doing. Preserve a healthy respect for Satan's activity along with a confidence in the power of the name and person of

Jesus. But don't rush into conflict with the powers of darkness without thorough preparation in confession, prayer, fasting and in company with other Christians, otherwise you will be playing with something as dangerous as a hand grenade —you never know when it will go off.

Further, if you have had any personal contact with occultism in any of its forms, repent of your involvement specifically and ask for cleansing and deliverance through the blood of Christ. Then put on the whole armor of God, stand firm, and be strong in the Lord and in the power of *his* might.

C. Schisms. These are divisions, particularly divisions for inadequate reasons, within a church fellowship. These were a problem in the early church, notably in the church at Corinth. Since those first days of Christianity there have always been two main dangers for believers. One is unity where there ought to be division, the other is division where there ought to be unity.

Unity where there ought to be division. A favorite Scripture text is John 17:21 " . . . that they may all be one;" but the context of this verse is a unity *based on truth.* In John 17:17-19 Jesus prayed, "Sanctify them through the truth; thy word is truth . . . and for their sake I consecrate myself, that they also may be consecrated in truth."

Here Christ was praying first and foremost for his apostles who were already agreed about the essential truths and doctrines. He was praying that they might not be divided over *secondary* matters. But there can be no true unity when there are basic differences over essentials of the faith, such as the deity of Christ, the atonement, justification by faith, the resurrection of Christ, the necessity of new birth or the authority of Scripture.

Division where there ought to be unity. Have you heard the parody of a famous hymn that goes like this:

> Like a mighty tortoise moves the Church
> of God;
> Brothers, we are treading where we've
> always trod.
> We are all divided, many bodies we;
> Very strong on doctrine, weak on charity.

There are at least five areas in which it is wrong for Christians to be divided. One is over *personalities.* An example from the New Testament is the "I belong to Paul, I belong to Cephas" mentality. A pervasive cult of personality is flourishing today with Christians moving from church fellowship to church fellowship, from convention to convention, not because of the absence or presence of life and truth but because they want to be near their favorite Christian personality.

Division over *positions of influence* is just as wrong, as exhibited by Diotrophes, who liked to be first, or James and John, who asked for positions on either side of Christ's throne in heaven.

Dividing over *social status* is wrong, paying attention to a rich man—"Have a seat here, please," —while ordering a poor man, "Sit down there" (James 2:1-7).

Spiritual gifts are likewise a wrong issue over which to divide. You may have one gift. I may have another. But neither of us should be jealous or proud. We are members together of the one body of Christ.

Finally, it is wrong to divide over *minor doctrinal issues,* no matter how crucial you or I may feel them to be. No one person has a complete monopoly of all aspects of God's truth. We all "see in a mirror dimly." Certain vital issues bind together all those who know and love the Lord Jesus; but in many peripheral areas my personal feelings and convictions may be strong but I cannot say I *know* I am right and all others are wrong. That is a characteristic attitude of the flesh (the feeling that everyone else is wrong except those in my own little group). Take prophecy, for example: you may be a pre-millennialist, a post-millennialist or an a-millennialist. Or you may not have the faintest clue what a millennialist is! But how ridiculous to let the devil divide us on such matters as these! We need a certain amount of humility, not bigotry, when it comes to these secondary matters.

If Satan were forced to choose one weapon only out of his total arsenal, it would probably be schisms. Consider this: nothing convinces the un-redeemed world more effectively that they should reject Jesus Christ as Savior and Lord than the sight of squabbling Christians. In that marvelous prayer of our Lord in John 17 to which I have already referred, we are reminded that the *purpose* of Christian unity, as Jesus prayed to the Father, is "so that the world may believe that thou has sent me" (John 17:21).

In other words, if Satan can keep Christians divided from each other, the world will be justified in doubting that Jesus is who he claims to be. No matter how orthodox the doctrine it preaches, no matter how evangelistic the program it conducts, a split or divided church is not a witness for Jesus Christ. Every unresolved quarrel between Christians is preventing the answer to Jesus' prayer.

None of this means that we must be unanimous about our ways of expressing our faith. It does mean that we must be unified in our allegiance to the Lord Jesus and in our loving devotion to each other's best interests—literally, *for his name's sake!*

Notes

[1] C. S. Lewis, *Screwtape Letters,* (Great Britain: Collins).

[2] Corrie ten Boom, *Defeated Enemies,* (Christian Literature Crusade).

[3] Cited by F. J. Rae, "The Expository Times," Vol. lxvi, p. 215.

[4] "Christian Science Journal," January 1901.

[5] James Philip, *The Christian Warfare and Armour,* (privately printed).

[6]From a sermon on Counterfeits, given by Dr. Martyn Lloyd Jones in Westminster Chapel, February 26, 1961.

[7]Kurt Koch, *Occult Bondage and Deliverance,* (Kregel, 1970).

[8]*Ibid.,*

Passages for further study: Exodus 7:11-12; 8:17, 18; 22:19; Leviticus 19:26, 31; 20:6, 27; Deuteronomy 18:10-14; I Samuel 28; II Kings 17:8, 17, 18; 21:1-6; 23:24, 25; I Chronicles 10:13, 14; Isaiah 2:6; 8:19, 20; 47:9-15; Jeremiah 27:9, 10; 29:8-14, 21-23; Ezekiel 13:17-23; Zechariah 10:2; Malachi 3:5; Matthew 7:13-23; 12:22-28; 24:24, 25; Mark 1:34; Luke 4:40, 41; 8:26-33; 11:24-26; Acts 8:9; 16:16; 19:19; Galatians 5:20; II Timothy 3:8; Revelation 21:8; 22:15.

Battle Orders

4

"Put on the whole armor of God . . ." *(Ephesians 6:11).*

Wars are not won on parade grounds or in brief-ing rooms. Neither can God's troops expect to fulfill their commission during a church service or at a Bible conference. The time comes when a disciplined and well-trained army must take to the battle-field, assault enemy strongholds and engage in hand-to-hand combat.

For this situation of intense strife and struggle, the Lord of hosts has designed both the suitable equipment and the successful strategy. Any Christian who rushes off to confront the enemy without God's equipment is a fool doomed to de-feat. Why? Because Jesus, our Captain, said: "Apart from me you can do nothing (John 15:5).

Do you suppose that may be a slight exaggera-tion? Surely, although we need the Lord's help to accomplish something really difficult, there must be other exploits which we can and should attempt on our own. But no. Jesus is quite defi-nite: *anything* of value in the sight of God is as dependent on his provision as a vine is dependent on its root.

Injuries

One of the surest ways to begin learning our utter weakness and helplessness without Christ, as I have often found in my own experience, is to be knocked around in the heat of battle and to suffer serious wounds. Even the apostle Paul, stalwart fighter that he was, had to learn the hard way that he was powerless in himself. In 2 Corinthians 12 he expressed his elation over the rare visions that God had granted him, only to be battered mercilessly afterward by a "thorn in the flesh," "a messenger of Satan." In the midst of his misery, as he cried to God for deliverance, the divine answer overwhelmed him: "My grace is sufficient for you, for my power is made perfect in weakness." So Paul came to this conclusion: "I will all the more gladly boast of my weaknesses, that the power of Christ may rest upon me. For the sake of Christ, then, I am content with weaknesses, insults, hardships, persecutions and calamities; for when I am weak, then I am strong!"

Or, of what use is an electric light that is not plugged into its socket? You might try plugging it into a physics textbook which describes electricity, or into promotional leaflets from the Electricity Board, but it will never light up from them! The Christian has only one power source and that is Christ himself. If we are not *connected* to him, we will not give out the light he intended, no matter how decorative we look or how high our wattage rating.

Jesus meant *exactly* what he said: "Apart from me, you can do nothing." Paul knew that in the deepest way when he wrote: "Put on all the armor which God provides" (Ephesians 6:10, *New English Bible*).

1. Our Equipment

When David, the shepherd boy, set out to confront Goliath, he nearly collapsed under the heavy, complicated coat of armor provided for him by King Saul (1 Samuel 17:38, 39). Explaining that he was not accustomed to such equipment, he advanced, instead, with his shepherd's staff, his slingshot and five stones. Watching his approach, Goliath felt so insulted that he ridiculed David. The boy replied "You come to me with a sword and with a spear and with a javelin, but I come to you in the name of the Lord of hosts, the God of the armies of Israel whom you have defied" (1 Samuel 17:45, 46).

What strange and cumbersome equipment some Christian soldiers attempt to take into battle —committee plans, publicity campaigns, organizational schemes. Is it any wonder that they bend under the weight of it all, or trip over its complexities? Obviously, we need to think in terms of an "outfit" radically different from the world's fashion. We need God's battledress.

Before we examine Paul's list of equipment given in Ephesians 6, three vital details need to be recognized.

Our "Achilles' heel"

First, God provides no protection for the back! The Lord intends for us to *face* the foe and fight. If we turn and run, we are on our own: " . . . if he shrinks back, my soul has no pleasure in him," says God (Hebrews 10:38).

From my own experience, I would say that a backslider, one who isn't facing up to his Christian commitment, is a most miserable and unhappy person. Sometimes a Christian flirts with the world, thinking that he is enjoying the best of both options. In reality, he is getting the worst of it—too much of the world to enjoy Christ fully, too much of Christ to really give himself to the "fleeting pleasures of sin" (Hebrews 11:25). Remember, if you get careless, the enemy will gladly shoot you in the back. He knows that is where you are unprotected.

Second, the *whole* armor is needed. One part may protect the heart but not the head; another the head but not the heart. We need every single piece of God's armor. We cannot pick and choose what appeals to us.

In the classic Achilles legend, the great hero was laid low by an arrow that pierced the only spot not covered by his charm of invincibility—his heel. The devil is a sharpshooter. Leave off just one piece of your spiritual armor and he will certainly aim for that vulnerable spot.

Third, some equipment is worn all the time, in readiness, while some is used particularly in the thick of the fight. Concerning the first three pieces mentioned, Paul uses a perfect participle, indicating a past action with continuing effects: "*having girded* your loins . . . *having put on* the breastplate . . . *having shod* your feet." These comprise the basic uniform of the Christian soldier. For the remaining three, Paul uses the present tense: "*taking* the shield . . . *take* the helmet . . . and the sword." These are special battle gear.

Here is the picture: a soldier is sitting in his tent waiting for the battle call. He has on his belt, his breastplate and his boots. Suddenly the bugle blows. He seizes his shield, clamps on his helmet, graps his sword, and moves out, ready for the enemy.

Now we need a more detailed discussion of the armor of God.

A. *The Belt of Truth.* Once, when I was in the Army, I remember our Sergeant Major on the parade ground suddenly turning to a new recruit shouting, "Jones, you're stark naked!" We all looked around to see this amazing sight. Jones was, in fact, quite normally and properly dressed, but he had forgotten to put on his belt. Because a belt holds on the other garments and keeps them together, it is vitally important not to forget the belt of truth.

Your whole Christian life should be "held together" with truth. You cannot live on feelings and experiences alone, however precious they often may be. You must live on the solid, objective truth of God's Word. How? First, by *knowing the truth*. That is why in all Paul's epistles we find very solid doctrinal teaching coming before the practical application of it. He is saying in effect, "This is our position in Christ. Now, act in the light of it. Become what you are." Some Christians do not know what they are in Christ, and therefore do not know what to become or how to become it. Remember that in Romans 6 Paul keeps on saying, "Don't you know? Yes, we know! We know! You must consider. . . ." Don't despise doctrine. If you have no belt of truth, you cannot possibly keep the rest of the armor in place.

Let me illustrate the practical importance of this belt by looking at some verses in the last part of Romans 8. Remember, the devil is always trying to undermine our confidence in the Lord. He is the great accuser. In Romans 8:31 and following, we can see this belt of truth as God's answer to four common accusations. The devil says, "You can't cope with your situation." But in verse 31 Paul replies "What then shall we say to this? If God be for us, who is against us?" When the devil comes again and says, "You're not a real Christian; look at your life," Paul answers in verse 33 "Who shall bring any charge against God's elect? It is God who justifies." The devil says, "You're a total failure!" But Paul asks, in verse 34, "Who is to condemn us? Is it Christ Jesus, who died, yes, who was raised from the dead, who is at the right hand of God, who indeed intercedes for us?"

Again the devil charges, "God doesn't love you," and in verses 35 and following Paul replies, "Who shall separate us from the love of Christ? Shall tribulation or distress...? For I am sure that (nothing)... will be able to separate us from the love of God in Christ Jesus our Lord."

A young missionary going out on her first term of missionary service to her mission field was sent into a remote part of the country to live with an older missionary who had become spiritually "fossilized" and hardened in her ways. The older woman made life, from the very first moment, almost impossible and intolerable for the younger, and this girl, within a matter of days, began to feel resentful and bitter that God had put her in this situation. She realized that her entire missionary work and calling was at stake. What could she do?

She decided to pray for the older missionary every day, and every day she read, on her knees, 1 Corinthians 13—the great chapter on love. That, for her, was the belt of truth which she put on, day by day. At the end of a whole year of praying and reading this chapter she had been given such a love for this older, hardened companion that the older woman broke down—overwhelmed by the love of her young friend. The whole situation was transformed because of the belt of truth.

We conclude that we must not only know the truth, *we must also show the truth*. There must be a most obvious sincerity and integrity about our lives. The truth of God's Word should be demonstrated more in our lives than from our lips. I was recently struck by some words of the Rev. Duncan Campbell: "The greatest thing about us all is not what we say, it is not only what we do; the greatest thing about us all is our unconscious influence, and that unconscious influence impregnated by the life of Jesus."[1]

"Not merely in the words you say,
Not only in your deeds confessed,
But in the most unconscious way
Is Christ expressed."

Some Christians live double lives—angels at church, devils at home! How many of us have some secret sin that is spoiling that unconscious influence for Jesus? It may be something that we dare not tell any other person, something of which no one else knows, not even the members of our own family. We have not even told Jesus and confessed it to him. And because it is hiding in the core of our lives, undealt with, we are devoid of that unconscious influence—the fragrance of Christ in our lives.

I believe, too, that the belt of truth suggests also a readiness for the battle. We must have the ABC of the Gospel at our finger tips, ready to be expressed to someone in desperate need of Christ. If someone stopped you today and said,

"Excuse me, could you please tell me how I can find Christ?" would you be ready and able to lead that person, step by step, into a new relationship with the Savior? Do you know at least six Bible verses which could show that person what God says about human sin and God's cleansing and salvation? For those who are not sure that they are equipped to do this I have suggested a simple framework in the Appendix on page 149.

B. *The Breastplate of Righteousness.* This piece of God's armor reminds us that we must be living a life that is right with God and right with man. Both our vertical and our horizontal relationships should be clear and true. Paul says in Acts 24:16, "I always take pains to have a clear conscience toward God and toward men." This is vitally important because if my life is not right with God and with man, I have no "breastplate," and I am very vulnerable indeed. I meet Christians from time to time who are having severe doubts. Perhaps the "fire" has died down in their lives and there is little real love for Jesus left. Often this is caused by sin and disobedience. Somewhere in those lives exists some thought or deed which needs to be repented of and confessed. Perhaps there is bitterness or resentment toward another person. Something has soured their life and spoiled their relationship with Jesus, corroding their breastplate until it has become useless.

I remember once having a huge boil on my

back and I was quite depressed about it. I had lots of sympathetic Christian friends who suggested, "Perhaps Satan is attacking you! You're right on the front line and you've become a special target of the Enemy." It was flattering to be told that, but I knew what *God* was saying to my heart and conscience. He was reminding me of unconfessed sin. I had been disobedient. I had lost my breast-plate and become defenseless. God was using that unpleasant experience of the boil on my back to waken my conscience until at last I confessed the sin and was right with God again. Now, please don't conclude from this illustration that every time you get a boil or a backache there is something wrong in your life! Just remember that some unpleasant experiences are hints from the Lord that something is wrong, something needs to be dealt with. We need to ask the question, "Lord, what are you saying to me in this?"

You see, faith and obedience go hand in hand, and if there is disobedience, I may claim God's promises, I may plead the name of Jesus, I may go to prayer meetings—when what I really need to do is listen to God and obey him. "If I cherish iniquity in my heart, the Lord will not hear me." Indeed, though James gives us the promise, "Resist the devil and he will flee from you," he *begins* by saying "Submit yourselves therefore to God. Resist the devil and he will flee from you. Draw near to God and he will draw near to you. Cleanse your hands, you sinners, and purify your hearts, you men of double mind" (James 4:7-8). It is only as our life is right with God that we can resist the devil with any conclusive and obvious results. Because, when our life is right with God, he gives us the perfect righteousness of Christ—our glorious breastplate.

C. The Boots of the Gospel. "Having shod your feet with the equipment of the gospel of peace. . . ." Roman soldiers wore heavy sandals, equivalent to the army boots of today. In part this means obviously a readiness and eagerness to preach the Good News: "How beautiful are the feet of those who preach good news." When I was in the Army, the first thing I did after strenuous training exercises was to take off those heavy boots and put on some comfortable slippers instead. But there are far too many Christians today who are part of the "bedroom-slipper brigade," who prefer to stay at home by the fire and watch their favorite TV program. Of course, they might be willing to share their testimony of Christ if someone happened to call. But putting on their boots and infiltrating enemy territory is another thing altogether. The early Christians kept their gospel boots on all the time. It was tough going. They were persecuted. Many of them shed blood. But if they had taken off those gospel boots the church would have died away in the first century, and you and I would not have been Christian believers today. If the Communists had taken their boots off in 1917, the Revolution would have gone no further than Moscow. But they kept their boots on, and now one-third of the world is under Communist control.

Moreover, the Roman soldier needed these boots for two main purposes. First, they helped him to *stand firm;* they kept him from slipping and sliding on difficult terrain. And that is a quality that is vital in Christian warfare—"to stand firm." There are a great many "nice" Christians, who will say and do what others want them to say and do; who will agree for the sake of being agreeable. They are men-pleasers, "yes men." They have no ability to stand firm. And with the pressures of today's world and the influence of false or fuzzy thinking and teaching, some Christians today slip and slide all over the place. "Stand firm!" says Paul. Put on those boots.

The boots also increase our *mobility*. They enable a soldier to move quickly and fearlessly over rough, unfamiliar ground. I believe that we Christians need to learn a lot about being mobile in a rapidly changing situation in society. Not that the Gospel should change. It is immutable. But our presentation and our approach should be flexible enough to dovetail with people's needs and situations. One lesson I am having to learn all the time is that you cannot continue in a rut, using antiquated methods and old-fashioned language, which were designed for a completely different generation.

D. *The Shield of Faith.* "Above all, taking the

shield of faith, with which you can quench all the flaming darts of the evil one." These flaming darts were flame-tipped arrows, and there was usually a barrage of these before the main assault —the "artillery" firing before the infantry went in. Flaming darts represent fierce, sudden and unexpected attacks. What are your first waking thoughts in the morning? Be honest! What do you think about first thing on Monday morning when the alarm goes off? I know what my first thoughts are like when I am tired and have a very busy day ahead; but I am learning to take up the shield of faith: "Thank you Lord for this new day. Praise the Lord! Lord Jesus, how wonderful you are!" Sometimes I lie in bed for a few moments quietly rejoicing in the Lord; I know too well how first waking thoughts can be pretty negative.

A friend of mine was host to a travelling evangelist, and when he brought him an early morning cup of tea he tiptoed quietly across the bedroom where the man was sleeping. Suddenly the evangelist sat bolt upright in bed, threw his arms up and said, "Praise the Lord!" My friend almost dropped his teapot! Over breakfast later he said, "Forgive this personal question, but do you always sit up in bed and say 'Praise the Lord' like that?" He replied, "Yes, I have learned that so often the devil attacks my mind and imagination before I even get out of bed, so now I take up the shield of faith first thing." (I advise that you warn your wife or husband before you do that tomorrow!)

Again, you may find sudden and unexpected persecution, or illness, or a wave of depression. Perhaps you have been praying for guidance and you experience sharp attacks of doubt afterwards. Recognize these as attacks of the enemy—fiery darts—and lift up the shield of faith as your sure protection.

E. The Helmet of Salvation. This head armor is designed to protect our minds and our whole attitude towards our Christian faith. If Satan cannot succeed in damaging us in other ways he will try to make us tired, discouraged and disillusioned. You will find questions like this in the Psalms, again and again—"*Why* do the wicked prosper and the righteous suffer?" What is the answer? Take up the helmet of salvation! Paul declares in Romans 8:18, "I consider that the sufferings of this present time are not worth comparing with the glory that is to be revealed to us." He looks ahead to the future glorious salvation when at last we shall see Jesus face to face, and then all the sufferings of the present existence will be forgotten in that first moment's welcome in heaven.

Sometimes in the midst of a battle, a Christian may be temporarily cut off from his own fighting unit. Suddenly he sees himself surrounded by enemy forces, exposed to all the perils of Satanic attack. At such a moment the devil may suggest this: "You thought you were saved, but look at the mess you are in now. You might as well surrender to me, because all that teaching about your soul's security in Jesus is just nonsense."

When the tempter comes with such evil insinuations against God's grace, the helmet of salvation will "keep your head on straight," will clear your thinking about the trustworthiness of God's promise to save you to the uttermost. Don't rush into battle without your helmet of salvation firmly on your head!

F. The Sword of the Spirit. All the pieces of God's equipment thus far have been protective, designed for the Christian's defense. This now is the weapon for attack, God's Word—the Spirit's sword.

How does this differ from the belt of truth which is also God's word? The belt is basic doctrinal knowledge that makes clear God's purposes for us and his program for accomplishing it. He wanted to redeem his sin-spoiled creation so he sent his Son, the Lord Jesus Christ, to accomplish that, and commissioned all believers in him to be special agents for the spiritual conquest of the world.

The sword, in contrast, refers to specific biblical teaching and understanding applied to particular battle situations. It requires a detailed knowledge of the Bible, committed to memory so that it is readily available for taking immediate offensive action against Satan. Every verse of God's Word that you have "hid in your heart" is a potential sword thrust to put the devil to flight.

It is "potential," because the word cannot be employed effectively apart from the Holy Spirit. It is *his* sword. The Word without the Spirit is lifeless legalism, as Jesus pointed out. A spirit—whether of zeal, of courage, or of anything less than the Holy Spirit himself—without the Word (God's definition and standard of truth) could lead to dangerous emphasis on isolated or individualistic "spiritual experiences" instead of the steady and balanced flow of God's power in our human lives.

The combination of the Word *and* the guidance of the Holy Spirit, however, is the sword that effectively drives away Satan and all his hosts.

As the army of the Lord marches into battle, it is perfectly equipped by God for protection and attack. Yet uniforms and weapons do not, by themselves, do the fighting. That is the soldier's responsibility. He must *use* what God has provided, and use it prayerfully. This calls for strategy, which God has planned for us as well.

2. Our Strategy

It is not enough to have battle equipment; we must also have a battle plan. God has drawn up his campaign against Satan with three components that will insure victory.

A. *Planned withdrawal*. This may come as a shock to those who think that we are to be ceaselessly charging forward and endlessly shouting victorious battle cries. The Word of God is quite clear in showing the importance of periodic rest and renewal in order to keep our forces at peak fighting efficiency. Our Commander does not mean for us to go into battle exhausted and weak.

Jesus said to his disciples: "Come away . . . and rest awhile" (Mark 6:31). He understood the prophet's word that "they who wait for the Lord shall renew their strength" (Isaiah 40:31). He knew the experience of weariness from doing battle all day against sin with its devastating effects in people's lives. Often he himself withdrew, alone, to pray (see Mark 6:46; Luke 5:16; 6:12). He also felt the personal necessity of preparing for a day's battles by spending time in quiet with God his Father (Mark 1:35).

Since prayer was so important to the Son of God, how dare we think that we can get by with less? Our "daily devotions" or "quiet time" are indispensable for renewing spiritual energies in the Lord's presence. Communion with him "polishes" the weapons of our faith.

The psalmist describes the Lord as "a strong tower against the enemy" (Psalm 61:3) and "our refuge and strength" (Psalm 46:1). This is not the language of retreat or of giving ground to the enemy. Rather, it is recognition of our need for a place where we can find our restoration.

My wife has found this lesson of great importance in recent years. At times she has felt very depressed (living with me, of course, this is not surprising). But she has learned, increasingly, to "run into this strong tower of the Lord" and to close the door. There she finds that the Lord gives her supernatural strength as she rests in him.

Let me give you another illustration of this "strong tower." On one university mission a young man came up after a meeting and asked to see me the next day. We set a time, and when he came he brought a girl with him. As she entered the room I had the most overpowering sense of evil—a cold, clammy, horrible feeling that made me reel. I gripped the side of the table next to me and in that moment of sudden fear, I "ran away to Christ." Quickly and silently I claimed the power of his name, and instantly the fear left me. I was able to counsel them and discovered that she was a practicing medium. We need, at times such as this, to make a strategic retreat, to run away for a moment into Christ, and there find our strength to resume the battle.

In my first parish we had a glorious mission taken by that lovely Dutch Christian, Corrie ten Boom—a wonderful child of God who has personally taught me so much of value. At the end of the week three of us who were leaders in that church went down to the station to say goodbye to her. Corrie got onto the train and we were left on the crowded platform. As the train began to pull out of the station, dear Corrie wanted to leave us with something to remember. She leaned out of the window and called to us in tones perfectly clear for all to hear "Don't wrestle; just nestle!" I think we proper Britishers all went a little pink. But I have never forgotten it. The emphasis in a Christian's life is not to struggle but to rest in Jesus. There is indeed a fight, but it is a fight of faith, as we rest in the Lord.

B. Unyielding Resistance. Repeatedly in Ephesians 6, Paul summons us to "stand" and "withstand" (verses 11, 13, 14). There can be no doubt that Satan means to keep the pressure on us. Remember, though, how desperate he is. The territory doesn't belong to him in the first place, and he knows that he is doomed to be driven out. With every device of his devilish imagination, he tries to fool us into thinking that the outcome is uncertain and that his forces are taking over. Have you ever been tricked into believing that as you read daily headlines about evil and corruption in this world? The enemy seems to have a lot going for him.

Once we start thinking like that we become tempted to surrender, or at least to give up and leave the field to the demons. The Word of God thunders at us: "Never!" The clarion command is "Resist the devil and he will flee from you" (James 4:7).

Satan, you see, for all his pride and guile, isn't really brave; he is simply brazen. He flaunts his disobedience in God's face, and he taunts God's soldiers about the unsophisticated simplicity of their faith (even as Goliath scorned David). But all the while he believes in God and shudders before God's truth (James 2:19). When he is resisted, in the name of truth, he runs.

How do we resist? By putting on the armor which God provides and by defying the claims and challenges that issue from hell.

God has wonderfully taken us out of the kingdom of darkness into the kingdom of light, from the power of Satan into the power of God. In so far as we understand our freedom in Christ, and believe it and act upon it, then indeed we shall experience our freedom; because in this realm of Christ, Satan has no right over us at all. Oh, he may shout at us and we may listen to him, and we may do what he wants. But we *need* not obey him! Certainly the devil will try to make us doubt our position in Christ. He will say "You think you are free, you think now that you're dead to sin and alive to God. But look at your experience! See how bound you are by selfishness and pride and temper and lust. You're not free at all—you're bound!" The devil is the father of lies. In his very first temptation he said to Eve, "Has God said . . .?" Are you quite *sure*? Constantly he tries to undermine our belief and conviction in the Word and the promise of God. He will do the same here. He'll say "You're not free. You're not dead to sin, not at all. You're very much alive to it." But we must hold on to God's Word. We must learn what it means to resist the devil when he attacks like this, until he flees from us.

I remember the vicarage garden in my first parish. Sometimes small boys from the neighborhood would slip in to take apples and pears from our fruit trees. The vicar's son, then about five years old, would stand in the garden with his hands on his hips and shout to the much bigger and tougher boys, "Get out of here. This is not your garden!" He had the authority to say that. And we have the authority to say to Satan, "Get out of my life. I don't belong to you. You have no right to dominate me because now I'm a child of God. I'm in Jesus Christ and I'm not your property. Sin no longer reigns in my life. Grace reigns. Get out, in Jesus' name!" And he *will* disappear.

C. All-out Attack. A common coaching philosophy in sport is: Attack is the best method of defence. In a football match the defence do their best to keep the ball out of their goal area. But when a good defender gets possession, his objective is to head for goal and to do everything he can to enable his team to score.

God's team is in possession. When Jesus died and rose again, he took the ball away from Satan. Not every attack a Christian makes will end up in a goal. Sometimes the ball may even end up behind his own line because the enemy's defence has won through. But remember; it was only the enemy's defence: The ball is in the Christians' hands. God will win the game.

We Christians should never be content to simply "hold our own," in our personal lives or in the life of the church. We have been handed the sword of the Spirit by which to rout the devil. We should be constantly on the offensive, reclaiming enemy-held territory for the Lord.

I asked a Christian the other day, "How are you?" He looked at me gloomily and answered, "Well, all right at the moment." as though just waiting for something to go wrong. I have noticed in my own life how easy it is, when someone says "How are you? Are you all right?" to reply immediately, "Oh, I had a terrible night last night. No sleep at all" (or whatever misfortune it might be). We forget about the countless blessings we have had. We tend to think about the one thing which may have been difficult. We need to cultivate the positive.

I was once helped by a little tract called *"What do you say?"* by T. L. Osborn. He begins, "You said you did not have faith, and that moment, doubt arose like a giant and bound you. Perhaps you never realized that, to a great extent, you are ruled and shaped by your words. You talk failure and failure holds you in bondage. You talk fear, and fear increases its grip on you." The answer? We must fill our hearts with "Thus saith *the Lord*". Then, we must confess that Word until it becomes a part of our nature. Hold on to the promises of God.

In wearing the right equipment and employing the right strategy, we must not forget for a minute that in all things we are totally dependent on the Lord himself to supply all of our needs. Only the power of the Holy Spirit within us enables us to "fight the good fight of faith," and thus assures us of being on the winning side. We must be strong *in the Lord.*

Some people are strong on doctrines, but doctrines themselves will not help us. Some Christians are strong on methods, but methods sometimes get in the way. It is only the Lord who can give us the victory.

Jesus *meant* it when he said, "Apart from me you can do *nothing.*" What the apostle Paul learned about Jesus is equally true: "I can do *all things* in Christ who strengthens me" (Philippians 4:13).

Now, onward to victory!

Notes

[1]Duncan Campbell, *The Price and the Power of Revival,* (Great Britain: The Faith Mission).

Victory Guaranteed

5

"Whatever is born of God overcomes the world ..."
(1 John 5:4).

Styles of warfare have changed from one historical epoch to another—from foot soldiers to cavalry to armoured tank division to pushbutton-controlled intercontinental ballistic missiles.

The Christian battle has never changed, but it has always been uniquely different from the conventional patterns of any other earthly conflict. Paul put it clearly: "For though we live in the world we are not carrying on a worldly war, for the weapons of our warfare are not worldly but have divine power to destroy strongholds" (2 Corinthians 10:3, 4).

Worldly warriors?
Yet a great deal of Christian activity would seem to parallel a "worldly war." We have a problem in the church—so at once we set up a committee. We have an objective—so at once we begin to plan our strategy. Someone has said, "I was hungry and you formed a committee to investigate my hunger. I was homeless, and you filed a report on

the indigent. I was sick, and you held a seminar on the situation of the under-privileged. You have investigated all aspects of my plight, and I'm still hungry, homeless and sick." Jesus would not smile at our parody of his charge. The trouble is that when we discuss things in committee (as we must, to some extent) the great temptation is to think as men think and not as God thinks.

An emergency meeting of church leaders was called because of some crisis in a certain church. The chairman, at the outset, stood and prayed with great fervor to an "Almighty and Eternal God whose grace *is* sufficient for *all* things" and then immediately introduced the topic for the meeting. "Gentlemen," he said, "the situation in this church is completely hopeless. It is beyond redemption. Nothing can possibly change it!"

Remember the stinging rebuke that Jesus gave to Simon Peter, when Peter meant so well and was trying so hard? Jesus had just spoken about his coming sufferings on the cross and Peter burst out, in sympathy, "Heaven forbid; no, Lord, this shall never happen to you." Jesus turned and said to Peter, "Away with you, Satan, you are a stumbling-block to me. You think as men think, not as God thinks" (Matthew 16:22, 23, NEB).

Do you see why he had become a stumbling-block to Jesus? Although he was thoughtful and considerate he was thinking like a man, not like God! Our war is not over geographical boundaries or economic issues or social crises, although as good citizens we are rightly concerned about such matters. As God's people, however, our primary engagement is with the spiritual powers of his enemy, Satan, who fights to rob God of glory by destroying human souls. That makes a difference in how we fight the battle as well as in its outcome.

1. Secrets of Winning

In any competitive enterprise, everyone wants to know how the other person achieves success. Christians have at least three almighty forces in their favor.

A. The Power of God's Word. We have already seen what an awesome piece of equipment is the Word. Jesus demonstrated that during the temptations in the wilderness after his baptism. In head-on confrontation with Satan, the Lord parried every devilish suggestion with a sword thrust of Scripture (he quoted verses from Deuteronomy 6 and 8). Knowing that he had met more than his match, the tempter departed.

If you expect to get the best of Satan you must *know* the Word of God. The devil can quote Scripture, too, you know, in order to confuse or trick us. He tried that with Jesus. A single Bible verse taken out of its setting has often been turned to the enemy's advantage. Half-truth is an effective deception. Christian fighters should make it a steady habit to memorize many Scriptures to increase and reinforce their knowledge of "the whole truth and nothing but the truth."

B. *The Authority of Jesus' Name.* When a soldier's action is challenged, his best defense is to name the officer who issued the orders he is obeying. It is not enough to be sincere and diligent; his action must be authorized.

Christians are on active duty by command of God the Son, Jesus Christ. Frequently in the New Testament, we see the impact that his name produces: for salvation—Acts 4:12; for authority—Luke 10:17, 19; for prayer—John 14:13, 14; for the Holy Spirit—John 14:26; for healing—Acts 3:6; for power—Acts 8:12; for everything—Colossians 3:17. The Holy Spirit has revealed that the name of Jesus is infinitely superior to any other on earth, and that one day every knee shall bow at the mention of it (Philippians 2:9, 10). With that kind of majesty, the name of Jesus cannot be trifled with or used carelessly.

The sons of Sceva, a Jewish high priest, tried using Jesus' name like some charm or magic formula, only to have the evil spirits they were addressing hurt and humiliate them (Acts 19:13-16). Jesus himself had warned earlier that some would employ his name at their own discretion instead of at his direction, with the result that he would disown them on the Judgment Day, even though they might have done many good works (Matthew 7:22, 23).

The rightful use of the authority of his name belongs only to those who have a genuine relationship with Christ. Those who humbly trust him as personal Savior and faithfully take their orders from him as their Lord—they only can act with his assured backing. Do we meet those two requirements that entitle us to use his name against Satan?

C. The Effect of the Cross. John's vision of the great future events in heaven explains the downfall of Satan "by the blood of the Lamb and by the word of their testimony, for they loved not their lives even unto death" (Revelation 12:11).

Christ Jesus, whom John the Baptist pointed out as "the Lamb of God, who takes away the sin of the world" (John 1:29), defeated the devil when he died on the cross and then arose from the dead. From that point on, God's eternal plan was clear; sinners could be saved from their deadly peril and restored to happy companionship with their heavenly Father forever by accepting his sacrifice for them instead of trying to atone for their sins themselves. The enslaved human spirit was now free, not only to enjoy God but also to spread that Good News to every lost sinner on earth!

But this becomes a dangerous enterprise because it threatens Satan's control. I was speaking at a missionary conference with Brother Andrew, and he told a very striking story of his last visit to Vietnam. He was travelling on a bus with a Christian in that country. As the bus stopped momentarily, a man with a basket walked in front of the bus. Suddenly the Christian said, "Watch out! There might be a bomb in that basket!" Brother Andrew asked, "Why are you so afraid?" His friend replied, "Well, that man might be a Vietcong. He might throw himself and the basket at the bus. He's not afraid to lose his life. But I am!" Brother Andrew commented: "That is just the trouble with Christians today. They are not willing to lose their lives for Jesus' sake; but there are countless people in the world today who *are* willing to give their lives for the sake of communism or for some other ideology. But how many Christians love not their lives to the death?"

You may know this challenge from a communist: "The gospel is a much more powerful weapon for renewal of society than is our Marxist philosophy; but all the same it is *we* who will beat you. We communists do not play with words; we are realists, and seeing that we are determined to achieve our objective we know how to obtain the means. How can anyone believe in the supreme value of your gospel if you do not practice it, if you do not spread it, if you sacrifice neither time nor money for it? We believe in our communist message and we are ready to sacrifice everything, even our lives. But you people are afraid to soil your hands." Christ's victory on the cross cost him his own blood.

On the cross, of course, Christ not only dealt with our sin problem, he dealt with Satan himself. There, at Golgotha, he "disarmed the principalities and powers and made a public example of them, triumphing over them in him" (Colossians 2:15). Although we are contending against powers infinitely more damaging than flesh and blood, Christ has rendered them powerless on the cross. The cross is a place, not only of desperate conflict and agony, but of ultimate triumph. Satan hates the preaching of the cross of Christ! And no wonder, because through Christ's death "him who has the power of death, that is, the devil" has been destroyed, and "all those who through fear of death were subject to lifelong bondage" have been delivered (Hebrews 2:14). Further, one verse in particular has often given me encouragement when it comes to this battle. John, in his first letter, tells us that "the son of God appeared to destroy the works of the devil." In Greek, this really means that he came to "untie" or "undo" the works of Satan. He tries to tie us up in knots, hundreds of them; but Christ is able and willing to untie all those knots and set his people free.

My daughter, when she was a little girl, sometimes came to me with a terrible mess of string or yarn and asked, "Daddy, can you untangle it?" And Daddy had to sit down for half an hour to unravel the tangled clump. Just so, Christ comes to untie the knots that the devil has made of our lives. Remember, "greater is he that is in you than he that is in the world"! Never do we need to be afraid.

Although our mission of fighting on God's side may bring suffering, even physical death, that no longer matters, since earthly life has been transcended by eternal life, the present and future possession of every faithful follower of the Lord Jesus. The blood of the Lamb, willingly shed at Calvary, has doomed the devil, pulling the sting from physical death, and has guaranteed deliverance from both the devil and death for everyone who believes.

2. The Winner—In Person

Consider now this astounding fact about us as Christians. In the context of all that we have been discovering together about the Christian's warfare, we are at the point of supreme significance. Resulting from the Incarnation, the Crucifixion, the Resurrection, and the gift of the Holy Spirit, three words announce this stunning truth: *Christ in you.*

Even the apostle Paul, with all of his learning and literary eloquence, seems to run breathlessly short of adequate words when he writes about it: " . . . the riches of the glory of this mystery, which is *Christ in you,* the hope of glory" (Colossians 1:27).

For all else that could be said about the mystery (which means a hidden truth now revealed), let us simply say that "Christ in you" is the Holy Spirit living in each believer to reproduce Christ's life. God—the Father, Son and Holy Spirit—is *one*

God. The Holy Spirit is the Spirit of Christ. Don't allow yourself to be side-tracked by attempts to explain or illustrate the mystery of the Trinity. It is a truth that transcends both reason and imagination.

The Victor in us!

But we are not focusing on theology about the Being of God here. We are revelling in the divine fact of "Christ in you." Do you realize the consequence such a truth holds for this battle against Satan which you and I are commissioned to fight? It means that Jesus himself is continuing his victorious conquest over the devil in and through *us* daily! We are not doing his fighting for him. Rather, we are sharing in his victory over the enemy's last-ditch defenses. Jesus is Victor—and he is on the scene in person—in *us!*

With that in mind, let's take a fresh look at the power of the Holy Spirit—Christ in us.

Even after Christ's resurrection the disciples were still, for at least six weeks, timid, frightened and uncertain about how they were ever to carry out their commission to be witnesses to Jesus. They knew the Word of God, they believed in the name of Jesus, they trusted the blood of the Lamb, but they still had none of the power and authority that they desperately needed—until the Holy Spirit came upon them. Often I meet with Christians who have given their all to Jesus but who have never received all that Jesus would give to them.

> The grand thing the Church wants in this
> time is God's Holy Spirit. You all get up
> plans and say, "Now if the Church were al-
> tered a little bit it would do better." You
> think if there were different ministers or
> different church order or something differ-
> ent, then all would be well. No dear friends,
> it's not there the mistake lies. It's that we
> want more of the Spirit. Now people are say-
> ing, "This must be altered and that must be
> altered," but it would go no better unless
> God the Spirit should come to bless us. You
> may have the same ministers and they
> should be a thousand times more useful for
> God if God is pleased to bless them. This is
> the Church's great want. And until that want
> be supplied, we may reform and reform and
> still be just the same. All we want is the Spirit
> of God.

Words like these might have been written for the
'80's, but in fact they were spoken by Charles
Spurgeon on August 31, 1857! Billy Graham has
put it like this, "The time has come to give the
Holy Spirit his rightful place. We need to be bap-
tized with the Holy Spirit; we need to know what
Paul meant when he said 'Be filled with the
Spirit.' Give it any terminology you like, we need

to accept it, to get something, for we do not have the same dynamic impact that the early Church had." Don't get "hung up" on terminology—whatever we call this ministry of the Spirit, we need it. Therefore I want to ask two questions:

A. *What does it mean to be filled with the Spirit?* Often there is some confusion on this point. What are you looking for if you are seeking to be filled with the Spirit? Is it a certain type of experience, something you have read or heard about? Several years ago, for a period of three or four months, I was in some distress of soul, longing to know the power of the Holy Spirit and to be more effective in my ministry. I read stories of revival, how the Spirit would come down and a person would be thrown to the ground by the Spirit's power, or suddenly in the middle of the night he would leap out of bed and shout "Hallelujah!" for four hours.

Well, I was waiting for something to happen, but I never jumped out of bed in the night. I'm not suggesting that we should be afraid of experiences if they are based on God's Word. You cannot possibly read the Acts of the Apostles without seeing that they had a great *experience* of the love of Jesus and the power of the Holy Spirit. However, the devil can tie us up in knots by urging us to seek a certain type of experience that we have read or heard about. God works in many different ways with different people. You need to seek *him*, and obey *him*, and yield to *his* lordship and get your eyes off what other people have experienced.

What, then, does it mean to be filled with the Spirit? In Ephesians 5:18 Paul gives us a clear command, "Be filled with the Spirit." This is not an optional extra; it is a command from God. But first, let me put this verse firmly into its context, to show that it is not just a "blessed experience." It involves at least seven elements.

First, it involves *walking in love:* "Therefore be imitators of God, as beloved children. And walk in love, as Christ loved us and gave himself up for us, a fragrant offering and sacrifice to God" (Ephesians 5:1, 2). He uses the phrase "imitators of God" because if we really are filled with the Spirit we shall have something of the divine image about us, especially this quality of love, because God *is* love.

It is interesting to notice that where, in the Acts of the Apostles, Luke says four or five times that "the Holy Spirit fell" on a group of people, the word "fell" is used in four or five other places in the New Testament in the context of an "affectionate embrace." We cannot build a doctrine on this, but it suggests that when the Holy Spirit "falls" on people, God gives them a loving embrace—they are overwhelmed by his love. That, I believe, was the essence of the power of Pentecost —they were so overcome by divine love that later Paul could say "the love of God controls us." And because they loved him with all their hearts, and because his love was constantly filling their lives, they grew in numbers and influence, like a swelling tide. People hated them, opposed them, persecuted them. But nothing could stop them, because of this overpowering love. Love is the hallmark of the Holy Spirit, and if anyone claims some blessing of the Spirit it is natural for us to look for two things—that Christ is glorified (for the Holy Spirit always brings Christ glory) and that there is love shown out of the life, because if there is not love, whatever else a person may have, he has nothing at all. In 1 Corinthians 13 Paul talks about tongues, prophecy, spiritual understanding, faith, generosity, self-sacrifice— all excellent things—but without love they are *nothing!* If we are to show signs of being filled with the Spirit, we must be walking in love.

Second, it means *walking in the light.* "For once you were darkness, but now you are light in the Lord; walk as children of light" (Ephesians 5:8). In other words, be in constant and complete fellowship with God, perfect not because *we* are perfect, but because the blood of Jesus goes on and on cleansing us from sin. As the tear water in the eye goes on cleansing its surface, so the blood of Jesus goes on cleansing us from sin. Of course, there must be a conscious and deliberate break with sin in your life. "Immorality and all impurity or covetousness must not even be named among you, as is fitting among saints . . . but instead let there be thanksgiving" (Ephesians 5:3 and following).

The Holy Spirit is a *holy* Spirit. God will not fill a vessel if it is unclean. If my wife asks me for a drink of water, I might go into the kitchen and pick up a glass. However, if it is not very clean, I do one of two things: either I wash it then and there, or else I put it aside and take another glass instead. In the same way, if God is going to fill a person with his Holy Spirit, either he must first cleanse that person (the result of repentance) or he will put that person aside for the moment and use someone else to fill the job he has to be done. The Holy Spirit is *holy*. There is no substitute for being clean in his service.

Third, if we are to be filled with the Spirit we must *praise and give thanks.* "Do not get drunk with wine, for that is debauchery; but be filled with the Spirit, addressing one another in psalms and hymns and spiritual songs, singing and making melody to the Lord with all your heart, always and for everything giving thanks in the name of our Lord Jesus Christ to God the Father" (Ephesians 5:18-20). What a wonderful picture! Joyful singing is, of course, always linked with times of spiritual revival and reality. It is the expression of someone who is so full of the Spirit that he longs to worship and praise and adore God. At Pentecost they said, "We hear them telling in our own tongues the mighty works of God." The 120 were full of praise! We should not be so cautious about experiencing God's love that we shy away from being "lost in wonder, love and praise."

In most churches we are much too frightened of emotion. I am an Anglican clergyman, and the Bishop of Coventry once said wryly: "Delirious emotionalism is not the chief peril of the English clergy!" Many of us are so staid and formal and correct—and dull! At Pentecost the crowd thought the disciples were drunk because of this wonderful "wine" of the Holy Spirit. Dr. Tozer once said that if Christians are forbidden the wine of the Spirit they will turn instead to the wine of the flesh. "Our teachers took away our right to be happy in God, and the human heart has wreaked its terrible vengeance by going on a fleshly binge from which the evangelical church will not soon recover, if indeed it ever does. Christ died for our hearts, and the Holy Spirit wants to come and satisfy them."[1] The heart that is full of the Holy Spirit will want to sing for joy. Moreover, praise is honoring to God and strengthening for ourselves—"the joy of the Lord is your strength."

Fourth, *right relationships* are a part of being filled with the Spirit. "Be subject to one another out of reverence for Christ" (Ephesians 5:21), and at once Paul goes on to speak of love and humility within Christian fellowship. Instead of pride, suspicion, jealousy or criticism, the love of Christ should so permeate our lives and fellowship that others will say, "See how they love one another." Paul immediately goes on to speak of husbands and wives: "Wives, be subject to your husbands, as to the Lord. . . . Husbands, love your wives, as Christ loved the Church," and so on. I would say that in marriage, the relationship between husband and wife is the most important thing after their individual relationship to Christ himself. In 1 Peter we are told that husbands and wives must watch this relationship or else their prayers will be hindered. However, other relationships are important as well, and Paul goes on to write about parents and children, about masters and servants.

Now, I think it is very significant that this question of relationships comes *immediately* after the command to be filled with the Spirit. A student missionary council did a survey of the causes of first term failures on the mission field. From a hundred missionaries who had been obliged to come home they discovered the main causes were these: inadequate devotional life—9%; failure to accept discipline—16%; inability to work with others—17%; feeling of superiority over natives —17%; friction between husband and wife—9%; lack of personal discipline—11%; other forms of laziness—17%; sexual problems—4%. Most of these problems indicate difficulties in personal relationships.

Briefly, Paul mentions three other matters in the context of being "filled with the Spirit": *spiritual warfare* (which we have already discussed in detail), *prayer* (Ephesians 6:18—"Pray at all times in the Spirit, with all prayer and supplication") and *boldness in witness*. (Paul asks them to pray "for me, that utterance may be given me in opening my mouth boldly to proclaim the mystery of the gospel, for which I am an ambassador in chains; that I may declare it boldly, as I ought to speak.") You will find this word "boldness" and similar words mentioned again and again in the early chapters of Acts. "They were all filled with the Holy Spirit and spoke the Word of God with boldness." The Spirit comes that Jesus may be glorified; the Spirit comes that we may be effective witnesses to Jesus. He does not come to gratify our personal desire for excitement.

B. How then can we be filled with the Spirit? Michael Griffiths says, in his book *Three Men Filled with the Spirit:*

> Our Lord taught (John 7:37-39) that the Spirit, when he is given, will well up in us like a bubbling spring to everlasting life (cf. John 4:14). Scripture also teaches that "God has flooded your hearts through his Spirit which is given to us" (Romans 5:5). If, therefore, we think of a fountain which is overflowing in such a way that it is constantly immersed, we have a clearer notion of what "the baptism of the Spirit" means. It is not merely a past experience but rather an ever-fresh experience of constant, total immersion.[2]

Let us look at some extremely important verses which speak of this—John 7:37-39: "On the last day of the feast, the great day, Jesus stood up and proclaimed, 'If any one thirst, let him come to me and drink. He who believes in me, as the Scripture has said, "Out of his heart shall flow rivers of living water." 'Now this he said about the Spirit, which those who believed in him were to receive; for as yet the Spirit had not yet been given, because Jesus was not yet glorified." I want to pick out from these verses four important verbs—Thirst, Come, Drink and Believe.

i) Thirst. "If any one thirst"—this is a selective invitation. It is not to everyone. But if you are thirsty to know the power of God in your life and to be an effective witness to Jesus, if you are thirsty for the fulness of the Holy Spirit, if you are thirsty to be the very best for God—*then* this invitation applies to you. And if you are *not* thirsty I would have to conclude that something is seriously wrong.

When I have been away on a mission I often bring home a small present for my son and daughter. If I say to them, "There's a little present in my study for you both," they go rushing in there, all eagerness to unwrap what I have chosen for them. I would think it very odd indeed if they showed no interest in what I had waiting for them, because they know how much I love them and want to show my love. And there is something seriously wrong if we don't want a good and wonderful gift that God has planned for us—because he loves us. If there is not that genuine thirst in our hearts, what is wrong?

It might be *ignorance* about the work of the Spirit. It might be *fear* of God, perhaps a fear that asks the question "What will God do to my life if I give him control?" Many Christians know little of the power of the Spirit in their lives because they are still standing in the shallows; they are afraid to get out of their depth. But it is only when God puts us in water deep enough to swim in that we really have to start *swimming!* That is when we begin to cry out to him, "Lord, I can't do it! Help! Without you I'll drown!" Our other fear might be concerned with what others think of us if we let the Holy Spirit take over our lives. We don't want to seem fanatics, or unbalanced. "The fear of man brings a snare."

Pride may also hinder our thirst. We may think we are quite all right as we are—*we* don't need any special blessing. One fine missionary to India in a former generation was a man who became known as Praying Hyde. As he left England for the first time on a ship bound for India, it was a momentous event for him. There he was, being sent out by the Lord. He had given everything to Jesus Christ. He was bound for a country at God's command. And as the ship began to sail, he opened a letter which a Christian friend had given him just before boarding. The letter said this: "Dear John; I shall not cease praying for you until you are filled with the Holy Spirit." John Hyde commented, "My pride was touched! I felt exceedingly angry, crushed the letter, threw it in the corner of the cabin and went up on deck in a very angry spirit. The idea of him implying that I was *not* filled with the Spirit!" Then he began to reflect on his reaction, and realized that God was not honored when he thought and felt like that. He went back to his cabin, and on his knees he searched for the letter he had thrown aside. He found it, smoothed it out and read it again and again. He said, "I felt annoyed; but the conviction was gaining on me that my friend was right and I was wrong. At last, in despair, I asked the Lord to fill me with the Spirit. And the moment I did this, the whole atmosphere was cleared up."

Of course there are many other things that might spoil our thirst for God—sin, resentment, a critical spirit, a wrong relationship. John comments that "the Spirit had not been given, because Jesus was not yet glorified." Although there is an obvious historical sequence hinted at here, there is also a spiritual significance to the remark. If Jesus is not glorified in some part of our life, the Spirit will not be given in all his fulness.

ii) Come. "If any one thirst, let him come to me," said Jesus. "To *me*." If you are thirsty, you don't go to the broom closet but to the water faucet. Jesus is the source of supply to meet our need, but we have to *come* to him.

When two men asked the Lord where he was lodging, he said: "*Come* and see" (John 1:39). When Andrew met Christ, he immediately found his brother, Simon Peter, and "brought him to Jesus" (John 1:42). When Nathanael skeptically questioned the authenticity of Jesus, Philip invited him to "Come and see" (John 1:46). Jesus cannot provide satisfaction for anyone who stays away from him. *We must come.*

Some people make an artificial distinction between Jesus and his Spirit. But the fact is that if we want to be filled with the Spirit we come to Jesus; and when we are filled with the Spirit, the Spirit makes Jesus more real to us. We find no awkward distinction, no conflict between the Spirit and Jesus at all. How could there be? As we come to Jesus for salvation, so we come to him for the power of the Spirit.

iii) Drink. This is where some people are confused. They go on asking and asking but never seem to receive. I went on for three to four months praying and praying to be filled with the Spirit and nothing seemed to happen. So I said, "Oh well, it hasn't happened today so I'll come back again and ask tomorrow!" And I went on asking to be filled with the Spirit, waiting for *something* to happen. But Jesus says, "If any one thirst, let him come to me and *drink*."

Suppose you came to my house one hot summer day and told me, "I'm so thirsty; could you give me a drink of water?" I would say, "Of course!" And then I'd get a glass and fill it up with water and give it to you with the words, "Here you are; this should quench your thirst." Then I might have to leave you for a few minutes. If, when I came back to you, you were still complaining of thirst because, although the glass of water was in your hand you had not drunk any of it, I would say, "Look. There it is in your hand. *Drink* it!" The illustration may seem ridiculous. How could any one behave so stupidly? Yet many people stop short at this very point with the gift of the Spirit. Paul tells us that God "has blessed us in Christ with every spiritual blessing in the heavenly places." We *have* everything in Christ. Therefore, Jesus said, "Now, drink! Receive!" It is simple.

iv) Believe. Jesus said, "He who believes in me, as the Scripture has said, 'Out of his heart shall flow rivers of living water.' " We must look at this carefully. The whole essence of faith is this, that if you have a promise of God, and you claim it, you must not only believe that it will be true but you must start praising God that it *is* true. Take the illustration of the Christmas story. When the angel promised to Mary the gift of a son, what did she do? She started to praise God that it was already true. She sang, in that tremendous anthem of praise, *The Lord has done great things for me*." If we had been there we might have said, "Mary, how do you know?" "Well, he's promised!" "Yes, but how do you *know*? You have no evidence at all apart from his promise. How do you *know*?" "Because he has promised!" You see, she started praising God the moment she received his promise to her. She had to wait for the actual fulfilment of the promise in her life, but she started at once praising God that it was already true. And as she continued praising, of course it became true, wonderfully true.

I have already described how I had asked to be filled with the Spirit. I asked again and again. I had the glass there in my hand, but I was not drinking and not believing. Eventually God opened my eyes and gave me the gift of faith to believe the promise I had known so well—the promise of Jesus in Luke 11:13: "How much more will the heavenly Father give the Holy Spirit to those who ask him!" I said, "Lord, I believe now; and I believe that I shall receive now and I will start praising you that you have now met my need, you have filled me now with your Holy Spirit." And as I started to praise him I had a most wonderful, quiet sense of joy and peace in the Lord. The precise nature of the experience is not important; it differs with different people. But we need to trust that as we come to Jesus and ask for this fulness of the Spirit, this power for witnessing for him, that he means what he promises.

Of course we must go on and on being filled with the Spirit. It is not a once-for-all blessing. We need to be refilled day after day. When Paul says, "Be filled with the Spirit," the tense of the verb means "to go on and on being filled with the Spirit." And as we *go on* believing in this glorious promise of Jesus, so from our heart will *go on* flowing those rivers of living water—providing our life is right with the Lord. Certainly we may sin and grieve the Spirit. But there is, praise God, the precious blood of Jesus to cleanse us again and the clear promise of Jesus to fill us again. And we can go out—feeling weak, perhaps, because in ourselves we are only empty vessels, but knowing that from our hearts, according to his promise, there will flow that living water, reaching out to the thirsty all around.

Are you filled with the Spirit? Are you thirsty? Will you come to Jesus? Will you drink? Will you believe? Will you thank and praise him?

Just before Paul's great discussion of battle orders in Ephesians 6, which we have examined so closely, the Apostle wrote: "Be filled with the Spirit" (Ephesians 5:18). The Reverend James Philip, who has written a very helpful commentary on Ephesians 6, says, "To be filled with the Holy Spirit is not the answer to the problems of the believer, but it is the signal for the problems and attacks to begin in earnest!"

And this is understandable. The fact remains that the more you long to know God and the more you long to be the best for God and the more you long daily to be filled with his Holy Spirit, the more you must train as a soldier of Jesus Christ because you will inevitably be plunged into the battle with God's enemy, Satan. We will really begin to know about the fierceness of the Christian's warfare only when we begin to know something of the blessed power of the Holy Spirit.

Praise God that the battle is not "to the death" but "to the life!" It is totally different from any other kind of warfare, using totally different equipment and strategy. Furthermore, because it is the risen Christ himself who is doing the fighting through his own Spirit, living in us as we have been reborn spiritually and recruited to join his side, this war has only one possible outcome: total destruction of the evil principalities and powers by the triumph of the cross (Colossians 2:15).

"Thanks be to God, who in Christ always leads us in triumph, and through us spreads the fragrance of the knowledge of him everywhere!" (2 Corinthians 2:14).

Onward, Christian soldiers!

Notes

[1] A. W. Tozer, *The Root of the Righteous*, (Christian Publications).
[2] Michael Griffiths, *Three Men Filled With The Spirit*, (Great Britain: Overseas Missionary Fellowship).

Appendix A

Some verses to help someone to find Christ:

A) Something to Admit:　　The fact of sin
　　　Romans 3:23 and 6:23
　　　Isaiah 59:2

B) Something to Believe:　That Christ has died for you
　　　Isaiah 53:5-6
　　　1 Peter 3:18

C) Something to Consider:　That Christ must come first
　　　Mark 8:34-38

D) Something to Do:　　Ask Christ into your life
　　　John 1:12
　　　Revelation 3:20

Appendix B

Verses for spiritual warfare:

I John 4:4　　　He who is in you (God) is greater than he
　　　　　　　who is in the world (Satan).

I John 3:8　　　The reason the Son of God appeared was
　　　　　　　to destroy the works of the devil.

I John 5:4　　　Whatever is born of God overcomes the
　　　　　　　world; and this is the victory that over-
　　　　　　　comes the world, our faith.

James 4:7　　　Submit yourselves to God. Resist the devil
　　　　　　　and he will flee from you.

Romans 6:11   Consider yourselves dead to sin and
                   alive to God in Christ Jesus.

Luke 10:19   I have given you authority to tread
                   upon serpents and scorpions, and over
                   all the power of the enemy; and noth-
                   ing shall hurt you.

Ephesians 6:11   Put on the whole armor of God, that
                   you may be able to stand against the
                   wiles of the devil.

Colossians 2:15   He disarmed the principalities and
                   powers and made a public example of
                   them, triumphing over them in (the
                   cross).

2 Corinthians 10:4 The weapons of our warfare are not
                   worldly but have divine power to des-
                   troy strongholds.

Revelation 12:11   They have conquered (Satan) by the
                   blood of the Lamb and by the word of
                   their testimony.

Hebrews 2:14-15   That through death he might destroy
                   him who has the power of death, that
                   is, the devil, and deliver all those...
                   subject to lifelong bondage.

I Peter 5:8-9   Your adversary the devil prowls
                   around... Resist him, firm in your
                   faith.

Romans 8:31   If God is for us, who is against us?

Romans 8:37   We are more than conquerors through
                       him who loved us.

I Corinthians 15:57 Thanks be to God, who gives us the
                       victory through our Lord Jesus Christ.

Messages by David Watson on STL Message Tapes

Finding Jesus
God's View of Sex
How God Guides Us

Five Bible Readings on 'The Christian Warfare'
1. The World
2. The Flesh
3. The Devil
4. The Armour of God
5. The Power of the Spirit

Five Bible Readings on 'The Church – The Body of Christ'
1. Its Purpose
2. Its Fellowship
3. Its Gifts
4. Its Ministry and Leadership
5. Its Witness

All these tapes are available from your local Christian bookshop or direct from STL Mail Order, PO Box 48, Bromley, Kent.

A complete list of STL Message Tapes will be sent on request to the above address.